Y

IN THE FIELDS
and the TRENCHES

★★★★★★★★★★★★★★★★★★★★★★

THE FAMOUS AND THE FORGOTTEN ON
THE BATTLEFIELDS OF WORLD WAR I

Kerrie Logan Hollihan

CHICAGO
REVIEW
PRESS

Published by Chicago Review Press Incorporated
814 North Franklin Street
Chicago, Illinois 60610
ISBN 978-1-61373-130-7

Library of Congress Cataloging-In-Publication Data
Are available from the Library of Congress.

Interior design: Sarah Olson

Printed in the United States of America
5 4 3 2 1

In memory of my grandfather
Frederick Urban Logan
US Army soldier and bugler in France
1918–1919

CONTENTS

* * *

This map depicts Europe at the outbreak of World War I.

GENERAL MAP
EUROPE IN 1914

SCALE OF MILES
0   100   200   300

Department of Art and Military Engineering at the U.S. Military Academy

PREFACE

✦ ✦ ✦

"COME AND DIE"

On Monday, June 29, 1914, newsboys on American and European streets shouted headlines to passersby with reports of an assassination far from home. The heir to the throne of Austria-Hungary was dead.

Archduke Franz Ferdinand and his wife, Duchess Sophie, were making a state visit to Sarajevo, Bosnia, a tiny province under the empire's control. As their open car rolled through Sarajevo, a 19-year-old Serbian revolutionary named Gavrilo Princip ran into the street and shot the couple point-blank. Princip, who dreamed of independence for his fellow Serbs, had no idea that he had set off a world war.

Most Americans and many Europeans didn't dwell on the killings. Bosnia, tucked into the southern end of the vast Austro-Hungarian Empire, seemed like a remote, unimportant spot. Ordinary Britons, French, and Germans had their own lives to think about. It was summertime, when young folks enjoyed a welcome break from their long, dark winters. Irène Curie, a French student who studied science at the Sorbonne in Paris, looked forward to her vacation at the seaside. A British university student, Ronald Tolkien, was writing letters to his fiancée

Shot to Death, proclaims the June 29, 1914, headline in the *New York Tribune*, reporting on the assassination of an Austrian archduke, the act that ignited World War I. *"Chronicling America," Library of Congress*

and inventing a fanciful language he named Elvish. A German student, Walter Koessler, was deep into architecture classes at his university.

Across the Atlantic, Americans read the news, too, but many of them had never heard of Bosnia or Serbia and knew little if anything about the imperial family of Austria-Hungary. Central Europe was very far from home—the voyage by sea alone from New York to the coast of France took more than a week. Proud to be citizens of a nation that had overthrown its king, Americans liked their independence and stayed wary of foreign entanglements, as President George Washington had advised so long ago. The United States and its people had no plans to entangle themselves in a European war.

That June, young Americans were enjoying the summer. A high school sophomore, Ernie Hemingway, was working a job at his family's summer home in the woods of Michigan's Upper Peninsula. Quentin Roosevelt, the 17-year-old son of a former US president, had friends coming to celebrate the Fourth of July with his family at Oyster Bay, New York. Buster Keaton, at 19, was a veteran comic making people laugh on New York's vaudeville stages. A Colorado cowboy named Fred Libby was working as a farmhand north of the border in Calgary, a city in western Canada. The troubles of European nations and their kings and emperors didn't matter to any of them.

No one could have predicted that in three years Ernie, Quentin, Buster, and Fred would be on European soil fighting for their lives. Irène, Ronald, and Walter would see war in France much earlier.

On July 28, 1914, exactly one month after Gavrilo Princip shot Franz Ferdinand, Austria-Hungary declared war on Serbia and set off a massive chain reaction that exploded into the Great War, what we now call World War I. There seemed to be no turning back, because Europe's nations were caught up in a tangled web of alliances. When one country went to war, the other members of its partnership followed suit.

Austria-Hungary's declaration of war lit a ring of fire that spread through much of Europe and the Middle East. Russia, allied with Serbia, mobilized its army on July 31 to fight the Austrians. On August 1, Germany, bound by treaty to Austria-Hungary, declared war on Russia to the east. On August 3, Germany declared war on Russia's ally France to the west.

By August 4 the German army was rolling across Belgium, a neutral nation, on its way to invade France. Across the English Channel, Great Britain, obligated by treaty to defend Belgium, declared war on Germany that same day. On August 6 Austria-Hungary declared war on Russia.

In just ten days, the ring of fire was fully lit. The imperial giants of Great Britain, France, and Russia aligned their forces to become the Triple Entente, soon known as the Allies. Japan joined them, and later, Italy. Germany and Austria-Hungary formed the Central Powers, aided by Turkey and Bulgaria. As global empires, each of these nations counted on its colonial armies to join them in battle. In the end, 32 countries fought in the Great War.

Chests swelled with patriotic fervor. Young men in Germany, France, and Great Britain rushed to enlist. Children, wives, and sweethearts lined the streets as ranks of their proud soldiers marched to railway stations, where troop trains waited to carry them to the front in France and Belgium.

Soldiers tucked pictures of their loved ones in their pockets, and many packed prayer books in their bags. As young men marched by, teenage girls darted into the streets to tuck flowers into the barrels of their rifles. Most of these soldiers—as well as their sweethearts, their mothers, and their governments—believed they'd be safely home in time for Christmas.

One young man didn't see things that way. The poet Rupert Brooke, already a star in England, wrote to a friend, "Come and die. It'll be great fun." Brooke did die in the war—not in battle but from an insect bite that went septic as deadly bacteria poisoned his blood.

At first, enthusiasm for combat ran high as old soldiers made battle plans and young soldiers enlisted to carry them out. Both sides expected the war to be short. But lightning fast, the Great War became a nightmare of blood and death in the trenches across Europe. On August 22, 1914, reality began to hit home when 27,000 French soldiers died on a single day. Over four years, 35 million people were killed.

A German soldier bids good-bye to a young woman holding flowers.
Library of Congress, LC-B2-3357-7

The governments and their generals were incredibly short-sighted. Soldiers on horseback were no match for machine guns and rapid-fire field artillery, both innovations since Europeans last battled in the 1880s. When the snow flew along the battle line of the Western Front, it became midnight clear that no one was coming home for Christmas.

President Woodrow Wilson shared Americans' isolationist feelings, and for two years the US government steered clear of Europe's conflict. However, hardened realists like former president Theodore Roosevelt warned that war with Germany was inevitable and begged for the United States to prepare.

Indeed, it seemed to many Americans that Germany was doing its best to entangle the United States. German submarines torpedoed British ships carrying American passengers, and other German subs were spotted lurking off the American coast. In early 1917, Germany's government warned the United States that its U-boats stood ready to torpedo American ships. By the spring of 1917, when an intercepted telegram revealed that Germany was trying to recruit Mexico as an ally, Americans had had enough. In April the United States declared war on Germany.

"Christmas in the field!" says this German poster printed in 1914. "Donate gift packages for our warriors!" Obviously, the war hadn't ended by Christmas of that year. The Germans would hang a similar poster in 1917.
Library of Congress, LC-USZC4-11707

Americans felt sure that their democratic ideals would defeat the German Empire. Their fighting men from the land of the free and the home of the brave would defeat the German Huns once and for all. Fresh-faced, well-fed, and filled with bravado, young Americans left cities and farms to fight the War to End All Wars. Rich and poor, black and white, rural farmhands and college men—all signed up to serve in the American Expeditionary Forces under the command of an American hero, General John Pershing.

Some young American women mobilized, too, taking over men's jobs in factories and on farms. A few sailed to France to serve as telephone operators, nurses, or workers for the Red Cross, YMCA, and Salvation Army. A handful of "girl reporters" managed to get to the front to cover the war and take photos in the trenches.

✳ ✳ ✳

Wars are fought by young people, and young people fighting wars make history—in ways great and small. This book tells the stories of 18 men and women who played a part in the Great War in Western Europe. They fought in battles, flew warplanes, killed the enemy, nursed the wounded, and fell in love. One died in combat. The rest came home, their lives forever changed.

Some of them had famous names, but most did not. Some had distinguished themselves in battle and returned as war heroes, while others would reach their prime as writers, businesspeople, scientists, and film stars. One became president of the United States. Another died penniless, estranged from his family.

These men and women lived a century ago. They felt altogether modern, and indeed, for the time they lived, they were. They encountered heroes, cowards, comics, and villains. They learned about human nature—power, greed, death, love, hate, courage, and fear. Like women and men of any age, they came away from a devastating experience with mixed feelings of despair, joy, hatred, loss, and hope. Their stories plainly show how they shared with us the tough journey that we call life.

TIME LINE

* * *

– 1914 –

June 28   Archduke Franz Ferdinand and his wife, Austro-Hungarians, are shot during a state visit to Bosnia.

July 28   Austria-Hungary declares war on Serbia.

August 1   Germany declares war on Russia.

August 3   Germany declares war on France.

August 4   Great Britain declares war on Germany. German forces invade neutral Belgium.

August 10   France declares war on Austria-Hungary.

August 12   Great Britain declares war on Austria-Hungary.

August 16   The British Army lands in France; Russians move into eastern Germany.

August 20   Germans occupy Brussels, the capital of Belgium.
Fred Libby enlists with the Canadian army.

August 23   Japan declares war on Germany.

September 6	First Battle of the Marne begins near Paris, France.
	Dick and Ethel Roosevelt Derby care for wounded soldiers in France.
September 15	First Battle of the Aisne begins in France.
October 20	First Battle of Ypres begins in the Flanders region of Belgium.
	Irène Curie begins work as an X-ray technician.
November 5	Great Britain declares war on Turkey.
	Theodore Roosevelt writes his book about the Great War.
December 25	Unofficial Christmas truce briefly stops fighting on the Western Front.

— 1915 —

January 19–20	Germany uses Zeppelin in an air raid on England.
	Walter Koessler is drafted into the German army.
	US president Woodrow Wilson declares American neutrality.
February 2	German U-boats attack Allied and neutral ships and blockade England.
April 22	Second Battle of Ypres begins as Germans launch poison gas on French.
April 25	Allies land in Turkey to launch the Gallipoli Campaign.
May 7	German U-boat torpedoes the *Lusitania*.
	President Wilson accepts Germany's apology for American deaths on the *Lusitania*.
May 23	Italy declares war on Austria-Hungary.
June	*Ted Roosevelt, Archie Roosevelt, and Dick Derby start military training in Plattsburgh, New York.*
	Ronald Tolkien takes honors and graduates from Oxford University.

August	Germany stops its unrestricted submarine attacks.
September 5	Czar Nicholas II takes command of the Russian army.
October 6	Austria-Hungary and Germany invade Serbia. *Ronald Tolkien trains with the Lancashire Fusiliers. Noel Denovan departs Australia to fight in France.*
December 28	Allies withdraw from Gallipoli after a futile nine-month battle.

— 1916 —

February 21	The Battle of Verdun begins in France.
April 9	Germany launches a massive assault at Verdun.
May 31	English and German ships fight the Battle of Jutland off Denmark's North Sea coast, with no real victor.
July	The Battle of the Somme begins in France. *Fred Libby moves to the Royal Flying Corps as an observer. Irène Curie sets up X-ray stations across France. Ronald Tolkien sees combat in the trenches.*
September 15	The British introduce tanks at the Battle of the Somme. *Fred Libby observes tank deployment from the air. Ronald Tolkien is hospitalized in England.*
November 13	The Battle of the Somme ends as one of the bloodiest battles in the war.
December	One million have died in the Battle of Verdun.

— 1917 —

January 16	Germany sends a coded telegram to recruit Mexico as an ally.
February 1	Germany renews its policy of unrestricted submarine warfare.

| February 24 | President Wilson learns about the Zimmermann telegram to Mexico, intercepted and decoded by British Admiralty Intelligence. |

February 24 — President Wilson learns about the Zimmermann telegram to Mexico, intercepted and decoded by British Admiralty Intelligence.

March 1 — The Zimmermann telegram is published in US press, sets off a nationwide demand for war against Germany.

March 12 — Moderates declare that Russia is a republic. *Fred Libby pins on pilot wings.*

March 15 — Czar Nicholas II abdicates the Russian throne.

April 6 — The United States declares war on Germany.

June — *Ted and Archie Roosevelt arrive in France.*

June 26 — First American troops in France.

July 31 — The Allies launch the Third Battle of Ypres.

August — *Eleanor Butler Roosevelt starts work for the YMCA in Paris.*

October 9 — Allies attack in the Flanders region, northern Belgium. *Fred Libby returns to the United States.*

October 23 — Americans experience trench warfare for the first time in the Meuse-Argonne Offensive.

October 24 — Austria-Hungary defeats Italy at Caporetto.

November 7 — The Bolsheviks seize the Russian government in a coup. *Lucian and Helen Johns Kirtland marry in New York.*

December 9 — Britain captures Jerusalem from Turkey.

December 10 — The Bolsheviks agree to an armistice with Germany.

– 1918 –

January 8 — President Wilson's Fourteen Points document sets framework for peace. *Dick Derby works in a French field hospital.*

February 18 — Germany invades Russia.

August 8	The British attack at Amiens, France.
September 12	Americans attack at St. Mihiel.
	Harry Truman and Battery D fight in the Argonne Forest in France.
	Christy Mathewson is injured during gas attack training.
October 4	Germany and Austria-Hungary make diplomatic contact with President Wilson.
October 25	Top German general Ludendorff resigns.
October 28	Italian army crosses the Piave River.
October 30	Turkey reaches armistice with the Allies.
November 3	Austria-Hungary surrenders and signs an armistice agreement with the Allies.
November	Allies reach an armistice agreement with Germany. Kaiser Wilhelm II abdicates the German monarchy. Germany establishes a republic.
	Buster Keaton and the Sunshine Company play for the troops.
November 11	The Armistice goes into effect at 11:00 AM.
	Harry Truman orders Battery D to stop firing.

– 1919 –

January	*Theodore Roosevelt dies.*
February	*Henry Lincoln Johnson marches in the New York City victory parade.*
March	*Katherine Stinson arrives home from France with undiagnosed tuberculosis.*
June 28	Peace treaty is signed at Versailles.
	Lucian and Helen Johns Kirtland photograph the crowds in Versailles.

THE COWBOY

* * *

FRED LIBBY

Frederick "Fred" Libby (1891–1970) was an American-born cowboy whose adventures and misadventures landed him in Calgary, a city in western Canada, just as the Great War broke out in 1914.

In the 1960s, an old man with the nickname "Cap" sat down to write his memoirs. Bent over with pain and a severely crooked back, he reflected on his first 26 years, "written from my heart." His memoirs interested a New York publisher, but as he was putting the finishing touches on his manuscript, he died, and his book of memories was set aside. He had called it *Horses Don't Fly*, and it seemed the book would never be printed until his grand-daughter brought it back to life. It was published in 2000.

"Cap" was Captain Frederick Libby, son of a Nebraska rancher who experienced more in those 26 years than most people who live three times as long. From schoolboy to cowboy to soldier to gunner to ace pilot, Fred Libby did it all.

Fred opened his tale with a description of his mother's death from tuberculosis when he was four. No one sat the little boy down to explain exactly what had happened, so he took in the news "sort of piecemeal," a little at a time. His much older sister and brother each took a turn helping to raise young Fred.

From the get-go, he was a handful. Fred's father delegated brother Bud to keep Fred alive until he turned 18, and if he did, their father would give Bud three of his best horses. On Fred's sixth birthday, his father gifted him with a saddle, bridle, and a pony named Slowpoke.

With Bud in charge, Fred learned the basics of horsemanship. Slowpoke, about the same age as his new master, allowed Fred to "ride him everywhere like we were real pals"—until the first time the pony threw him. Fred rode the devilish Slowpoke for two years until their "final battle" when he tried a circus trick with his pony and Slowpoke trampled him. Bud stopped Fred from going after Slowpoke with a small bat as payback.

Bud understood that small boys are best redirected out of their anger, so he offered Fred two unbroken ponies. "These new ponies are fast and tough and will stand no foolishness," Bud told him. "If you learn to ride them, you'll be plenty good. By the time you're ten, I may have a real cowboy for a brother." When Fred turned 10, he roped an antelope and was dragged under a picket fence, still wearing his brand-new Sunday suit. One look at his battered son, and Fred's father revised his bargain: Bud must keep Fred alive only until Fred turned 15.

Bud held up his end of the deal, and at 18 Fred was a high school graduate, expert horseman, and respected bronco buster. That winter of 1910, Fred left for desert life in Phoenix to recover from a heavy cough; his father feared the early onset of tuberculosis. But Fred arrived in Arizona cough-free and took a job breaking horses in the high desert above Phoenix, where a bronco ran him into a tree and broke Fred's leg.

With only an elderly Mexican cowboy on hand to splint the break with pieces of shingle, Fred endured an agonizing wagon ride back to Phoenix. To Fred's good fortune, they met friends on the way who passed him a bottle. "By the time we reach Phoenix in the daylight," he wrote, "I feel no pain and have no bourbon." Fred didn't know then how often such small gifts would help him through hair-raising, painful events to come.

Time and again, he'd lose all his money. Then some good person would loan him some cash or give him a job. When he lost everything in the first hand of a stud poker game in Colorado, Fred took a job watching over several thousand head of cattle, living alone with three cow ponies for company. A sudden October snowstorm trapped them all for the winter. Though hundreds of cattle died, Fred survived, dreaming that one day he'd move to Tahiti, a place he'd discovered in a magazine.

After that winter, Fred moved on. He and a buddy, Berry Carter, took a ship from San Diego up the coast to Seattle, then worked their way east and finally north across the Canadian border and east again to Calgary, Alberta.

The smell of money was in the air in Calgary, because nearby prospectors had struck oil. For Fred, the timing was perfect. He decided to invest. "This is the last of May," he thought, "and in July I will be a really old man of 22 . . . If [I] don't get rich soon, it's over the hill."

Eager Calgarians lined up to buy shares in the Pilgrim Progress Oil Company. Flush with cash, Fred and Berry each plunked down $500, and when they were told the stock was sold out they spent another $500 for shares in a different company. Certain they'd make a fortune in a few months, Fred and Berry took farm jobs with a family 30 miles away. They were still working the harvest on August 4, 1914, when World War I erupted in Europe.

On August 20, their farm work finished, they rushed to Calgary to see how their oil stocks were doing. They soon learned they had been swindled; Fred had spent $1,000 to own shares in oil companies that never existed.

Fred and Berry decided to head north for Edmonton and mining country. On the morning of September 2, 1914, as they breakfasted on waffles in Calgary, the air buzzed with news. Canada, a dominion of the British Empire, had military ties to Great Britain and was going to war against Germany.

> Calgary had gone nuts. Since five empires declared it the war has been on just a few days, but there are uniforms everywhere, as well as many recruiting offices. War has arrived with a vengeance. Canada is rushing to get a first contingent together. Still one hears from many sources that the war can't last, that Germany isn't strong enough. It's sure to be over by Christmas.

Eating waffles that morning changed Fred Libby's life. At the restaurant he and Berry met a recruiting sergeant who talked up life in the Canadian army—lots of travel, a ticket back home from the war, and a signing bonus to boot. Before he knew it, Frederick Libby, American cowboy, had signed up as a private in the Canadian army's 2nd Division with plans to drive a supply truck in the service of His Majesty King George V.

Armed with suitcases and outfitted in civilian clothes, Fred and 32 others marched to the station and boarded a private railroad car for Toronto, where they had to pass both a physical and a driving test. How Fred the bronco buster passed his driving test was questionable, because he was clueless about trucks.

Fred and his new buddies expected to ship out immediately for France, but the army took its time and spent six months training its raw recruits. "From all we can hear, the more training the better, as what started out to be a small battle is a real crisis and the first Canadians to go in action have taken an awful beating with horrible losses."

The Allies had learned the importance of training the hard way. In the first few months of war in France, the number of casualties staggered the imagination as Canadians joined the British to fight the First Battle of Ypres in Flanders (northern Belgium).

Fred's orders to France eventually came through, and in November 1915, under cover of night, the brand-new ocean liner–turned–troop transport *Metagama* docked in Liverpool, England. Fred's unit crossed England by rail, settled into a muddy camp for a time, and then it was on to France.

As he hauled supplies to the front in his truck, Fred never envisioned fighting, though he heard the battles rage.

> The war was coming closer . . . we could hear the roar of the big guns and meet ambulances on their way back to the hospital with their sick and wounded. Then the observation balloons began to show up and we met thousands of troops on the march, both going and coming. The ones coming had just left hell, those going were just entering hell, some for the first time, many never to return.

It was winter 1916, and as the rain poured down, Fred and the other men of his motor unit drove trucks with American names like Pierce-Arrow, Locomobile, Peerless, and Packard. Fred made one round-trip every night from base camp to supply depots near the front line, running his truck on narrow cobblestone roads, trying to stay in the middle. He was just as likely to slide into a ditch if he had to pass or make way for an oncoming vehicle. It was dark, with only a dim headlight shining on the road ahead. Any brighter, and the enemy could see him, too. He didn't drive all the way to the frontline trenches. That was a job for horses, which could traverse the muddy ground far better than any truck.

For wartime, it wasn't a bad job. "If we think we are in trouble," Fred recalled in his memoir, "we always try to remember the poor devils living in the trenches. With water everywhere, it is impossible to keep dry, and along with the weather there are the damn rats, cooties and, just a rock's throw away, our enemy, the Hun. The Germans seized the high (and dry) ground on a long chalk ridge, while our boys are dug in across from them in what had once been swamplands."

Matters changed one wet morning when Fred stopped to read a notice posted in the orderly room of his motor unit. As a buck private, he stood at the very bottom of the army's hierarchy, and he expected to spend the rest of the war driving a truck. But the notice offered a nearly unbelievable opportunity: to become an observer for the Royal Flying Corps (RFC), an officer's job at an officer's pay.

Fred applied—he'd do anything to get out of the rain. "True, I know nothing about aeroplanes or what an observer is supposed to do—but one thing I do know, they don't fly in the rain, and we've been living in rain for months." Fred figured that the RFC was in no hurry to bring him on, and he also assumed that it would take at least 30 days to train and receive his commission as a second lieutenant.

But the Royal Flying Corps was desperately short of flyers, a well-informed sergeant told him. "The Hun has more ships, more men, more everything, that is why they are scraping the bottom of the barrel for flyers." The sergeant's brute honesty appalled Fred, and he worried he'd acted on impulse. The RFC moved just as quickly. Three days later, orders came down for his interview, and he met with a colonel.

Fred answered the usual questions: did he have any experience with planes, what made Fred think he could fly, and so on. Then the conversation turned to horses. "What a horse has to do with flying I didn't know, as horses don't fly, but here I was on safe ground, so I assured the colonel I was an expert with horses. This pleased him more than I expected, as he was the owner of several polo ponies, and we had a nice discussion about horses in general."

The Royal Flying Corps snatched Fred Libby from the motor unit, and things moved fast. In mid-July 1916, he said farewell to his truck-driving pals and boarded a train at 7:30 in the morning. Three hours later he was on duty at the RFC's 23rd Squadron, in a field learning to shoot a machine gun.

Such was the job of an "observer" for the Royal Flying Corps. Fred would be a gunner, a sitting—and standing—duck, flying with a pilot in an open airplane over enemy lines, tracking and shooting down German fighters.

"What do you know about a machine gun?" came the gunnery sergeant's first question. That Fred knew nothing was no problem for the sergeant, who in 30 minutes taught Fred how to shoot the Lewis machine gun, the standard weapon that an RFC observer fired using two hands. His instructor then showed Fred how to climb into an airplane and maneuver the Lewis gun while flying.

A single ammunition canister for the Lewis gun held 47 rounds, which an observer could empty in a few rapid bursts of fire. The gunnery instructor, however, forgot to explain how Fred should change drums of ammunition while airborne, a key piece of information that nearly got Fred killed the same day.

Fred's squadron flew the F.E.2b, a "pusher" type airplane with motor and propeller mounted between a set of double wings, propeller behind the motor. The pilot sat in front of the motor with the observer in front of him. During combat, Fred, as observer, either knelt or stood in the nacelle (cockpit) watching for enemy planes in front or to either side. The Lewis gun was mounted so that Fred could swing it up and down and from side to side in a broad arc.

But if the enemy came up on their rear, matters changed. To fire behind him, an observer was required to climb up and stand on the airplane, with nothing to hang on to but a second Lewis gun mounted behind him. It seemed ludicrous to expect a gunner to work like this, but there was no other way to shoot an enemy closing in on his tail.

Fred's first training flight took place right after his 30-minute gun lesson. His target, an empty gas can, lay on the ground in the open airfield.

> I'm flat on my bottom for the take-off, then I'm supposed to either stand or get on my knees to be in position to shoot on our way back. This I am preparing to do, when he [his pilot, Captain Stephen Price] throws the ship in a steep bank to turn. I almost swallow my tongue and my eyes are full of tears, for I have no goggles, so we fly over and past the target. . . .
>
> As Price makes a second trip toward the target, I am in position with the gun pointed where I think the target will show up. This it does and I press the trigger and can see the petrol tin bounce and roll over—how could one miss with forty-seven rounds?

When Fred went to change the ammunition drum, it flew from his hand, caught the wind and just missed the propeller and the pilot's head. The gunnery sergeant had forgotten that part of the morning's instructions.

Frederick Libby wearing the uniform of a British officer.
National Museum of the Air Force

After lunch, Fred was outfitted with a new flying coat, goggles, and gloves. At 2:30 he reported for his first combat mission. Fred admitted to his pilot, Lieutenant Hicks, that he couldn't distinguish German planes from their own. Hicks assured him that a friendly pilot would "show his colors," and if he didn't, Fred was to "let him have it." There would be time the next day for Fred to study silhouettes of the German planes—the Fokker, the Roland, and the Albatross.

Six planes took off for a three-hour reconnaissance flight into "Hunland" (as Fred called German-controlled territory), flying a wide circle down toward the Somme River and crossing back in over the British front at Albert, France. Fred's plane was in position as the upper back escort, considered to be the toughest spot in the formation. He didn't know that at the time, but he realized later he'd been spared a lot of worry.

For the first hour of this first mission, Fred familiarized himself with landmarks on the ground—roads, towns, rail lines, and rivers. Sitting there in the nacelle of an F.E.2b, with machine guns front and back, Fred thought about the folks at home, his father and brother Bud in Colorado, and his darling Aunt Jo in Boston, where he had gone to high school for two years. None knew that Fred was now a gunner for the Royal Flying Corps. He asked himself why on earth he was here in France, when what he'd really planned on was moving to Tahiti.

Then the afternoon's work started, as the lead pilot, identified by strips of colored cloth tied to the struts of his airplane, took up his position at the front of their formation.

Captain Gray just sailed past with the streamers on his tail and the rendezvous is on. . . . The big ships fall into formation . . . and we are on our way toward Arras, where the trenches are well in view, and I can see in every direction for miles. . . . One can see into Hunland, far as the eye can reach.

Fred tried to calm his nerves, thinking about a good piece of advice Bud had given him. "Say, Pard, take it easy, don't be tense and if trouble comes, your muscles will tighten up fast enough in action." With the rest of their formation slightly forward and below Fred and his pilot, Fred suddenly saw—coming "out of the blue" from the right, directly at them—an enemy aircraft

out of which is coming what I take to be puffs of smoke, but which I learned later was tracer ammunition. Instantly I grab the Lewis which is resting in a clip on the left of my nacelle, throwing it over so I can get into action. In doing so I fall back with the gun on top, having missed the clip where I was supposed to anchor the Lewis. When I have kicked the gun off and into position to shoot, the Hun is almost directly in front of us and has gone into a vertical bank. There are two big iron crosses, one on each wing, with the body of the ship in between. Again I press the trigger of my Lewis and let the forty-seven rounds go, no aim, no nothing. I just shoot. I am not thinking, everything I did was automatic, as the Hun disappears from my view, going along about his business.

It was time to head back to base. Lieutenant Hicks knocked Fred gently on the head to get his attention and stuck out his hand to shake Fred's. Fred realized his first flight was "over in nothing flat. Nobody hurt, but I should be dead, certainly. The Hun's beaten me to the first shot, but my pilot didn't seem to mind, and why he was so pleased I couldn't understand."

When they landed, several airmen gathered at the hangar to greet the green observer. Clearly, something was up. Fred, in fact, had scored a victory. He'd shot down that German plane. "First flight, first fight, keep up the good work, because when they go down in flames they don't come back," his colonel proclaimed. Fred and his tent mate, Sergeant Chapman, celebrated

A pair of men in the Royal Flying Corps demonstrate how they work as pilot and observer (gunner) on the F.E.2b, a "pusher" type aircraft.
Wikimedia Commons

by going to a French home for a dinner of eggs and potatoes and a bottle of champagne.

Fred wasn't to share a tent with the sergeant for long. In 20 days' time he was recommended to receive a commission as an officer, second lieutenant with the RFC. During those 20 days, Fred thought hard about the Lewis gun and how an observer like him was expected to shoot. Because it took both hands, an observer couldn't stand steady, especially when he fired the rear gun while standing atop the airplane itself.

Fred came up with an ingenious solution: to place a butt stock on the Lewis gun. That way, an observer could steady the gun against his shoulder in the same way a hunter holds a shotgun. Now his left hand was free to hang onto the aircraft as he shot, holding the pistol grip with his right hand.

After a week's break in London, where he bought uniforms and learned to live the life of a British officer, Fred crossed the English Channel to join the 11th Squadron. It was late summer, and the weather was lovely for passengers on deck. Fred marveled at the variety of people on the boat—Hindus in colorful outfits, ministers of the gospel, Canadian nurses who were "snappy and beautiful in their officers' uniforms," RFC pilots and observers.

> But the most outstanding are the infantrymen going back to a hell on earth. . . . These boys have no illusions. Every day for them is just another day and tomorrow, if it comes, just another of the same. They are the poorest paid, the poorest clothed, the poorest fed, but are the backbone of the entire army and always fight under the poorest conditions. Thank God for the infantry.

Fred's "first big show" came as he and his pilot, Captain Stephen Price, escorted 36 bombers as they attacked German airfields in France. As they returned home, German airplanes filled the sky. The Germans never crossed their own lines, so every air battle took place over "Hunland." What was more, German pilots held a huge advantage because the Atlantic wind blew west, slowing the Brits' trip homeward.

Their squadron, in perfect formation, was attacked from two directions.

> We simply nestle down close to our lonesome bombers and pick the Hun off when they come in, and here's where my butt stock proves itself. . . . [It] is like shooting fish with the front gun held firm by the shoulder. Two bursts and he is upside down, then into a spin. I thought Price would jump out of our ship, he was so happy, but this was nothing. Almost to our lines, I catch a Fokker

moving to come up under the tail of upper back F.E.2b. Using the back gun . . . and holding the gun solid with my shoulder, I empty all forty-seven rounds in his middle. Two chances, two wins, two confirmed.

It seemed odd that if a British airman went down in German territory, he was said to have gone "west." When a British flyer crashed behind enemy lines, he was actually east of home. The truth was that if a British pilot had a choice, he'd rather crash-land far east of the German lines, where—if he survived—he'd likely be picked up by German airmen. There was an honor code among airmen of both sides, and a British pilot would likely be taken prisoner by the German air corps. Infantrymen were a different breed, and Brits tried their best never to crash near the German front, where trigger-happy German soldiers were all too ready to kill the British pilots who'd shot at them.

On July 1, 1916, French and British forces launched a huge offensive at the German army, a four-and-a-half-month struggle that became known as the First Battle of the Somme. Fred neatly explained the Allies' battle strategy:

Artillery has turned loose everything they have for both are old and new emplacements and when they raise their fire to hit farther back on the Hun's rear, our infantry will go over the top [scramble up and out of the trenches and attack the Germans on foot]. Our planes are everywhere, protecting our artillery.

The Battle of the Somme came to be one of the bloodiest of the Great War, both for the men on the ground and the airmen above. News reached Fred's group that 50,000 to 60,000 British soldiers were killed or wounded on the first day alone. Every night that summer, new faces appeared when the officers of the 11th Squadron sat down for dinner, replacements for the fighting

Germany's Kaiser Wilhelm II, nicknamed "Kaiser Bill" by Allied troops.
Edgar Allen Forbes, Leslie's Photographic Review of the Great War

men killed or taken as prisoners of war. The Battle of the Somme dragged on into November.

When Fred was temporarily assigned to a green, overambitious pilot, the man made a crazy attempt at glory by getting in a dogfight and nearly tossed Fred overboard. Those were a terrible few days for Fred, and he thought seriously about writing home to explain what he was doing. But there was no point in worrying his father. He wouldn't be going home after the war because he'd given up his American citizenship. He promised himself, "I shall join the Tahiti folks and grow bananas or something because they tell me this war is going to make the world safe for Democracy. . . . All we have to do is crucify the kaiser and his flying corps, and Democracy reigns forever. Whatever Democracy is I don't know."

Things got better when Fred was reunited with Captain Price. Fred Libby and Stephen Price were the senior duo in their squadron, with six enemy kills. Stephen, a gifted pilot, was far more capable than most others handling the big F.E.2b. Everyone looked forward to getting new airplanes with improved, synchronized guns timed to shoot through spinning propellers.

The British first put tanks into service along the Somme, and by mid-September Fred was officially reporting on their progress. At first, tank deployment was disastrous.

To say they [tanks] are something new would be very accurate. They were not only new to the German infantry but ours as well, and very new to some of the poor guys driving them. I saw one jumping along like an ant on a hot rock. He flopped from one trench to the other until free of the trenches, then started spinning around in a circle like something was wrong with his driving apparatus. Poor guy was in Hunland going around in a circle. What happened I don't know.

On September 17 an entire mission of airplanes went down, 12 men and six planes, the worst day on record for the 11th Squadron. "Tonight there will be 12 new faces at our dinner, and there should be six new machines in the hangars," Fred recalled. "All the flyers will undoubtedly be new and green. It just isn't possible to have any old-timers. There can't be any left. Dinner tonight will not be much, but the twelve new boys will have to be made welcome, for certain they are not going to be enthused with their future."

Fred Libby and Stephen Price's outstanding record and uncanny ability to outlive everyone else garnered them an unexpected honor. At one of those squadron dinners, their commander announced that they'd been awarded the Military Cross for their gallantry in service. Fred was stunned. He forgot his manners as his pilot and senior officer, Captain Price, came down to the junior end of the table to congratulate him. Fred didn't miss the irony of his own situation. "As a former American who has lost his citizenship, I wonder how Congress would like them apples." On their next return to London he and Stephen visited Buckingham Palace, where on November 14, 1916, a "very tired" King George, as Fred noticed, pinned the Military Cross on Fred's best uniform.

During the winter of 1917 Fred learned to fly, and in March he pinned on his pilot's wings. He tucked his observer's wings in his pocket; they meant the world to him and represented the good luck he'd had. He returned to France as a member of the 43rd Squadron, flying a Sopwith two-seater, Fred in front with a Vickers gun that he could shoot as he flew, and his observer just behind him. The flying was good; Fred's "little ship" was a delight to fly, and he relished sitting down in a cockpit out of the wind. But as much as he adored flying, the killing continued, and many of Fred's friends in the 43rd disappeared behind German lines.

The German pilots were under a new commander, an upstart named Baron Manfred von Richthofen (the "Red Baron") who painted his planes in wild colors and tagged them as the "Flying Circus." The Red Baron's predecessor, a gallant ace pilot named Oswald Boelcke, had followed the airman's code of honor by dropping lists of names of dead and captured pilots where the British could pick them up. But Boelcke was dead—killed in a midair collision. Fred doubted that the Red Baron's gang would show the same respect.

Then Fred's days flying with the RFC came to an end. The United States had entered the air war; the US Army was establishing a flying unit and needed seasoned pilots. Fred agreed to go home. At the American embassy in London, friends warned that he was making a mistake, that the US Army was so deeply mired in politics it would make him sick to his stomach on his first day home. Word was that the American general whom Fred so admired, a pilot named William "Billy" Mitchell, was the only officer "who knew anything about flying."

Nevertheless, in October 1917 Fred landed in New York, only to learn that his father had died just a few days earlier and would never know what his cowboy son had accomplished in France as an airman. When Fred got to Washington, the army major who met him treated him like a nobody. He was ordered to don an American uniform and remove his treasured wings—he'd have to prove his stuff by taking an old Curtiss Jenny for a test flight.

Fred learned he'd be lucky to qualify as a junior military aviator in the US Army Signal Corps. There was no official flying unit in the army.

Fred indeed felt sick. He'd made a terrible mistake, and he was caught up in a mess of military politics. General Mitchell, though a gifted pilot with a burning wish to create a real American flying corps, wasn't a graduate of West Point, the army's elite military academy. But West Pointers, with nary a pilot among them, commanded the flying branch of the Signal Corps. Fred cursed himself for ever leaving England and wondered what he'd gotten himself into. Fred Libby, ace pilot—and a US citizen once again—wound up in Texas for pilot training, American-style.

His back began to hurt, such horrid pain he needed medication. He ended up in a dirty, unheated military hospital outside Fort Worth, with no toilets or hot water. Only a handful of doctors, four nurses, and a few orderlies cared for more than 2,000 soldiers sick and dying from an assortment of contagious diseases: flu, spinal meningitis, measles, and pneumonia. "Fellows dying like flies," he recalled. At regular intervals, Fred dragged himself from his bed to keep a friend alive by clearing his sick buddy's breathing tube. There was no one else to help him.

An overworked but kindly doctor got him transferred to a better hospital, and from there Fred went to see a specialist in New York, who confirmed the bad news: Fred had a permanent, debilitating disease with a baffling name: ankylosing spondylosis.

Fred Libby, the British ace, would never fly for the Americans. All he could do now for the war effort was take part in a Liberty Loan fund drive at Carnegie Hall, where he auctioned off his streamers, the bits and pieces of the American flag that had gone with him as a pilot on his missions over France.

In fall 1918 a doctor ordered him to sunny San Diego, where the warm climate would be kind to his back. But when Fred got off the train, he was shocked to see everyone wearing flu masks. Influenza, the deadly virus that was killing millions of young people like him all over the world, had arrived in San Diego. Already in a weakened state because of his back, Fred caught a chill and went to bed. The chill turned out to be flu.

Flu patients were usually kept at home, but Fred put on his uniform and talked his way into getting a hospital bed. In early November, the fight for his life began, and on the evening of November 11, Fred lay close to death. Fever-stricken and barely conscious, he was still aware of the whispers at his bedside and the noise from outside that sounded strangely like a New Year's Eve party.

He made the turn that night. When he awoke the next morning, Fred's fever had gone, the sign that he would survive the flu after all. His nurse explained all that noise from the night before. Folks had been out celebrating. The war was over.

With some embellishment, Fred Libby's story ran in a comic strip in the 1930s. *King Features Syndicate*

Fred Libby left World War I permanently disabled, but his strong spirit carried him through a long, busy life. He went into the oil business and is thought to have founded Western Air Express, a precursor to Western Airlines. Keeping to his old habits, he made a fortune, and he lost it, too.

Over time, Fred's exploits were mostly forgotten. However, a photo taken at Edwards Air Force Base in the 1950s shows Fred, the World War I ace, posed with ace pilots who flew in World War II and the Korean Conflict. Fred was so hunched over he couldn't look up into the camera. Nonetheless, there he stood.

THE DAUGHTER

* * *

IRÈNE CURIE

Irène Curie (1897–1956) was the elder daughter of two renowned scientists, Marie and Pierre Curie. Irène turned 17 during the opening months of World War I.

In the summer of 1914, a teenage girl named Irène wrote to her mother in Paris from the small fishing village of L'Arcouest on the coast of northwest France. She spoke of how much she missed her mother and urged her to leave work and come join her and her sister, seven years younger, at the seaside. Irène and her mother hadn't seen much of each other over the past 18 months, but they were very close.

Her father was dead, crushed under the wheels of a delivery wagon in Paris in 1906. Her grandfather, who for so long had filled a spot in her heart, was dead as well. Her mother, so ill with a kidney infection (and on top of that a mental breakdown), was unable to care for the teen girl and her little sister. A Polish governess was now in charge of the girls' well-being.

The little family had often spent summer vacations in L'Arcouest, where Marie and her colleagues would take breaks from their work at the Sorbonne—Paris's famous university. But that easy friendship among families had disappeared; Marie had fallen in love with one of her married friends, and Paris newspapers had run her photograph, sparking a scandal that overshadowed all she had accomplished. Irène's mother, the Polish-born physicist whose work with Pierre had turned the science world upside down, was the world's best-known scientist, the first woman to win a Nobel Prize and the only woman to win the award in two different fields, Physics and Chemistry.

Despite the break from the intense year of university studies, Irène ached to be home in Paris with "Mé," her pet name for her mother. But in that summer of 1914, the clouds of war hung heavy on Europe, as Marie wrote to her daughters on August 1.

Dear Irène, dear Eve, things seem to be getting worse: we expect the mobilization from one minute to the next. I don't know if I shall be able to leave. Don't be afraid; be calm and courageous. If war does not break out, I shall come and join you on Monday. If it does, I shall stay here and I shall send for you as soon as possible. You and I, Irène, shall try to make ourselves useful.

The next day, August 2, Germany invaded France "without a declaration of war," Marie wrote to her girls. Soldiers poured onto trains to go into battle, yet, Marie noted, "Paris is calm . . . , in spite of the grief of the farewells." Though Irène begged in her letters to join her mother in Paris, Marie refused. No one knew what would happen. Irène and her little sister must stay safe on the coast.

On August 28, 1914, Marie wrote to Irène.

They are beginning to face the possibility of a seizure of Paris, in which case we might be cut off. If this should happen, endure it with courage, for our personal desires are nothing in comparison with the great struggle that now is underway. You must feel responsible for your sister and take care of her if we should be separated for a longer time than I expected.

With her secondary education complete, Irène had plans to begin her studies at the Sorbonne that fall. Irène expected to follow her mother's path. Up until now, she'd had an unusual education for a French child. Marie and her university colleagues frowned on the rote memorization and lack of physical exercise that marked France's education system, so Irène was among the 10 children who attended a cooperative school with classes taught by their parents. Every day, it was on to a different subject—Marie Curie taught physics on Thursday afternoons. By the time Irène was ready for the *lycée* (high school) she was thoroughly prepped in chemistry, math, experimental physics, literature, art, natural science, English, and German.

Marie Curie, Irène's mother and later, colleague.
Library of Congress

Marie hung a trapeze, rings, and a climbing rope in their garden so her daughters could exercise at play. The Curie family also got outdoors with biking and hiking trips, once with Albert Einstein, who talked physics with Marie and made the children "howl with laughter" when he stopped, took Marie's arm, and declared, "You understand, what I need to know is exactly what happens to the passengers in an elevator when it falls into emptiness."

The girls cooked, sewed, and modeled clay. They gardened, too. Marie adored plants and trees, even carrying packets of seeds in her wallet. When she supervised construction of the Radium Institute on the newly named Rue Pierre Curie in Paris, she installed lime trees and plane trees (similar to sycamores) the moment the building began to rise. She moved her equipment into the building, which became known as the *Institut Curie*, in the summer of 1914.

There, Marie continued her research looking for ways to produce radium at an affordable cost. Radiation was already used to treat certain types of cancer, and radioactive gasses "milked" from radium were thought to be useful in healing wounds. Doctors were just beginning to use radiation to help diagnose injuries such as broken bones. Some 20 years before, Wilhelm Conrad Röntgen had discovered X-rays, and his discoveries had been put to work in a few big hospitals in Paris.

As August unfolded, war broke out across Europe. For a time it looked as if the German army might invade Paris. Marie had a gram of precious radium in her laboratory, and she so feared losing it to the Germans that she packed it in a lead-lined suitcase and took it by train to another town for safekeeping.

Letters streamed back and forth from Paris to L'Arcouest. On August 29 Marie wrote,

Dear Irène, you know there is nothing to prove that we should be cut off, but I wanted to tell you that we must be ready for all sorts of alternatives. . . . Paris is so near the frontier that the Germans might very well approach it. That must not keep us from hoping that the final victory will be for France. So, courage and confidence! Think of your role as elder sister, which it is time you took seriously.

By early September, it was clear that the German army would not reach Paris, and Marie sent for her daughters. Eve started school, and Irène began to study nursing. Mé was forced to drop her research in her brand-new laboratory for a critical project that could not wait. August's battles left hundreds of thousands of casualties, and it became devastatingly clear that soldiers were dying for no reason but that they couldn't get medical treatment on the battlefield.

Marie Curie pondered that problem and quickly found her solution: she would bring X-ray equipment directly to the field. Begging, borrowing, and outright cajoling motor cars from well-to-do French, she equipped each with an X-ray tube, heavy glass

After a heavy rain, a Red Cross ambulance could get stuck in the endless mud. Often horses were most effective at dragging them out.
John Buchan, The Battle of the Somme

radiographic plates, and a dynamo (electric generator) powered by the car's gasoline engine. In weeks she had 20 mobile X-ray units rolling across France to battle zones—*Les Petites Curies*, "the little Curies," soldiers called them. One, a gray Citroën, she kept for herself, a Red Cross and French flag painted across both sides.

Eve Curie, who was only nine when the war came, went on to write about her mother's travels to the battlefields in a biography.

> A telegram or telephone call would notify Mme. Curie that an ambulance laden with wounded demanded a radiological post in a hurry. Marie would immediately verify the equipment of her car and attach her apparatus and dynamo. . . . She climbed in beside the driver on the seat exposed to the wind and soon the stout car was rolling at full speed—which is to say at the "20-miles-an-hour average" which was its best—toward Amiens, toward Ypres, toward Verdun.

Amiens, Ypres, Verdun—all were French towns whose names became infamous as battle sites where millions of soldiers died. Once at a treatment station, Marie set up her equipment.

> The melancholy procession began. The surgeon shut himself and Mme. Curie into the dark room, where the apparatus of action was surrounded by a mysterious halo. One after the other the stretchers laden with suffering bodies were brought in. The wounded man would be extended on the radiological table. Marie regulated the apparatus focused on the torn flesh so as to obtain a clear view. The bones and organs showed their precise outlines, and in the midst of them appeared a thick dark fragment: the shot or piece of shell.

That autumn of 1914, Marie recruited Irène as her very first "manipulator," her term for an X-ray assistant. Irène was only 17. At first, she traveled with her mother to both battle zones and hospitals, where Marie installed some 200 X-ray units. Marie worried that her child was too young to deal with the blood and gore of working on a battlefield, so she shielded her own feelings of horror at what she saw.

Not as well shielded was the X-ray equipment that exposed both mother and daughter to deadly levels of radiation. They took countless X-rays during the war years while standing behind wooden screens and wearing cotton gloves. Marie's raw, rough fingertips already hinted at decades of radiation exposure as she sorted through and cooked tons of pitchblende, a mineral ore, to extract its treasured radium. In 1936, Marie would die of leukemia, a cancer of the blood that was directly linked to radiation exposure. Irène, who carried on her mother's work at the *Institut Curie*, would also die of leukemia 20 years later.

Marie and Irène spent a year working together until mother was ready to let her daughter go solo, and Irène was left to move from one X-ray station to another all on her own. Already mature beyond her years, she now grew up even more quickly. After all, she was a very young woman working among surgeons and military officers far older than she. They were men with authority, and Irène could not claim the gravitas that came with the experience of an older woman like her famous mother.

At 18, Irène was serious-minded like Marie. She wore loose, comfortable clothes when her peers in Paris chose figure-fitting outfits, and she chopped at her curly hair herself. She had absolutely no worries about her appearance—or how she came across to others. She was known to be relaxed and fun around the other young people in her circle, but to outsiders she projected an awkward image. Her sister, Eve, wrote that their mother, despite giving her girls the best education she could, had somehow neglected to teach them the simple social graces—how to meet and greet strangers. In her life, Irène would meet many, and that awkwardness always hung with her.

Now on her own, Irène had to develop her social skills to get what she wanted. Busy bureaucrats and French military officers thought they could easily bypass the requests of a very young woman when it didn't suit them. But Irène learned that she could fight back by staying calm and making her case to a skeptical doctor or army official. When that didn't work, she acted on her own.

As she moved among treatment stations at the front and in hospitals, Irène also installed X-ray equipment. When she arrived at Amiens by rail, the city had just been bombed by German aircraft. Officials told her it might be two weeks until her apparatus could be set up. That didn't suit Irène, and she commandeered a sergeant and a medical student to move the

Irène Curie poses with a *petite Curie*, a mobile X-ray unit named for her mother, Marie. *Institut Curie*

delicate apparatus off the railroad car. In an hour she was organized and ready to work.

Daughter and mother exchanged letters constantly, Irène's full of news about her work and frequent compliments—and complaints—about the military doctors she worked with. From Montereau, France, in the summer of 1916, she wrote that she'd installed a *cabinet de photographie* (an X-ray machine) to screen a wounded soldier. His chest was so filled with fluid that standard testing was impossible. Irène's X-ray, however, detected several *projectiles* that Irène duly noted were "very difficult to see."

"Mé chérie," began the letter Irène wrote to her mother from a field hospital on September 13, the day after her 18th birthday. She'd used her X-ray equipment on a soldier's hand to locate four shell fragments so a surgeon could remove them. That afternoon, she'd taken a break to enjoy a soccer match, and that night, a small concert. She went to bed, as always in a tent, but on her birthday, she wrote, the sky was filled with stars.

Irène kept her wits about her. A message came from another X-ray station at Cabourg asking Irène for a favor. They'd damaged a coil, the message said, and they needed Irène to send her X-ray car to them. The suggestion appalled her, but she couldn't say why out loud: if she sent them her equipment, they could mishandle it and "destroy things in just a few days."

A few days later she wrote to her mother of a case when a surgeon used his fingers to probe for a bullet lodged in a soldier's leg. Irène, relying on X-rays to pinpoint the bullet's location, suggested to the surgeon that he make an incision in a different spot. It was clear to her the surgeon was old school and had no concept of triangulation. She knew what he didn't—using X-rays and simple geometry produced three-dimensional maps pointing to embedded bullets and bits of shrapnel.

In 1916 Marie established a training center for X-ray technicians at the *Institut Curie* and recruited women as radiology technicians. Irène, when she wasn't working at the front, helped her. She had never stopped studying at the Sorbonne, and she earned her degree the next summer. She also earned a French military medal for her work, but the government denied the same medal to her mother. Family legend said that, despite her heroism during the war, Marie Curie's reputation was still too tarnished after her love affair.

When the war ended in November 1918, Irène continued to train American officers in X-ray techniques, which they took home with them to the United States. A biographer wrote later that any flirtation "was met with a cold stare that was fueled by amazement rather than indignation." As ever, Irène was all business when she worked.

Still, Irène found a soul mate, and, like her parents, they too went on to work side by side. In 1925, she met the physical chemist Frédéric Joliot, her mother's new assistant. Irène and Frédéric married the next year. In 1935, the couple, sharing the joint surname Joliot-Curie, won the Nobel Prize in Chemistry.

THE WORDSMITH

* * *

J. R. R. TOLKIEN

J. R. R. Tolkien (1892–1973), a beloved teller of tales, is best remembered for his stories of Middle-earth. His book about small folk he called Hobbits was followed by a trilogy known as The Lord of the Rings, *which has sold millions of copies around the world and was made into a hugely popular film series in the early 2000s. He came of age and fought in World War I, and he never forgot what he saw on the battlefields of France.*

When John Ronald Reuel Tolkien was born in 1892, a trip by ship from his family's home in England to their new one in South Africa took three weeks. When he died in 1973, those 21 days had shrunk to 12 hours by jumbo jet. The years in between saw life change faster than anyone might have imagined at the turn of the 20th century. By 1973, Ronald (the name he went by) would live through two world wars, read in the papers that an atom bomb was dropped on Japan, watch televised launches of rockets into space, and marvel that a man could walk on the moon.

Ronald's own imaginary world lay in sharp contrast to the world outside his front door. He largely lived in his own head, a rich inner existence that he cultivated with care from the time he was a young boy. When he grew up to become a scholar and author, he shared his inner life with millions of readers everywhere in books printed in more than 40 languages. Their titles are household names. One is *The Hobbit*. Three more comprise *The Lord of the Rings*.

Ronald spent his first few years of life in South Africa. Like so many others in the heyday of the British Empire, his father, a bank clerk named Arthur Tolkien, had emigrated from England to the colony in the late 1800s in search of better work. The family didn't stay abroad, however; Ronald's father died in Africa when Ronald was three. His mother, Mabel had already returned to England with Ronald and his baby brother, Hilary. They lived quietly and without much money in a village in England's West Midlands. Mabel could just afford rent on the small cottage that shared a wall with one next door.

Ronald and Hilary had the freedom to wander where they wished, and they roamed the countryside to explore and play. Eventually, the lovely English landscape, which inspired so many artists and poets, would inspire Ronald, too, as he wrote about a magical, peaceful place he called the Shire. As the boys roamed and played, they were free to let their imaginations run wild—and to face a slew of imaginary foes. One was the Black Ogre, their name for an old farmer who chased the boys for picking mushrooms. Another they called the White Ogre, a dust-covered miller's son who frightened them away from the mill.

Ronald's mother became his first teacher, and she introduced him to Latin at a very young age. He was hooked on the ancient Roman tongue, both its sounds and its classic look on the page—yet another step in the life of someone who would become a writer. But soon enough, Ronald was ready to go to school, so his mother found them a small house in the smoky industrial city of Birmingham.

City life was hard. Mabel had taken the drastic step of leaving her Protestant roots in the Church of England to become a Roman Catholic in 1900, and she brought up her sons in her new faith. Mabel's conversion put her on the outs with her family, who refused to help pay her rent. The only housing Mabel could afford was just a step up from the slums, but to their good fortune, it was near the Birmingham Oratory, a church. In this community of Roman Catholic priests lived the kindly Father Francis Xavier Morgan, who befriended them.

Mabel Tolkien died in 1904 of diabetes, a death sentence in the early 1900s. Her orphaned boys lived in a state of benign neglect with an elderly relative for a time, until Father Francis stepped in and moved them to a boarding house where he could keep an eye on them and supervise their education.

At that boarding house Ronald met another orphan, a young woman three years older than he. Her name was Edith Bratt, and Ronald was enchanted with her. What free moments they had they spent together, and Ronald never looked further for a woman to love. Father Francis, however, thought differently. The priest ordered Ronald to drop the love affair, moved him and Hilary to another house, and forbade Ronald to so much as write a letter to Edith. Ronald honored Father Francis and obeyed him. Not until his 21st birthday would he reach out to Edith and rekindle the romance. Edith had moved on and was engaged to another man, but Ronald wooed her back.

Ronald was very bright and a good student, and Father Francis didn't object when Ronald was accepted into King Edward's School. Though it was not a Catholic school, it was among the best of its kind run by the Church of England. There Ronald met George Brewerton, an assistant master who drilled into his students the beauty of short, plain words in their native English. Years later, when Ronald spoke of Brewerton to his biographer, he looked back at his dynamic teacher. "If a boy employed the term 'manure' Brewerton would roar out: 'Manure? Call it muck! Say it three times! *Muck, muck, muck!*'"

Ronald also treasured his friendships with a circle of boys at King Edward's, Rob Gilson, Geoffrey Bache Smith, and Christopher Wiseman. All were great readers—and writers—of stories and poetry. They formed a sort of secret club, the T.C.B.S. (Tea Club, Barrovian Society). The boys based their group's name on the Barrow's Stores, which offered tea, coffee, and cocoa at cafés across the city. The four members of the T.C.B.S. made plans to do great things, and all four went on to university, a privilege granted to only a select few in the England of Ronald's day.

Ronald moved on to England's legendary Oxford, whose medieval towers, castle-like buildings, and gowned students and masters kindled Ronald's reverence for days long gone. He embarked on a study of the classics, all things Greek and Latin. But the many distractions of university life—rugby, debate, and hanging out with friends—proved more attractive than studying. He applied himself in just one class, an elective in philology, the study of literature and language. His professor, a robust, self-taught scholar named Joe Wright, introduced Ronald to the delights of Greek words. Wright also encouraged Ronald to dig deeply into the strange, consonant-heavy Welsh language, which had place names like Penrhiwceiber (pen-roo-KAY-ber), Senghenydd (sen-GEH-nith), and Tredegar (tre-DAY-gar).

With mediocre grades in every other class, Ronald finally figured out he was meant to pursue the study of philology. He switched from classics to a course in English language and literature and soon was digging into Old and Middle English texts. Fascinated with the songlike sounds of Welsh and the elegance of Finnish, Ronald spent long, quiet hours creating a complex language all his own. He eventually called it Quenya, and over the months, he worked to build Quenya into a spoken and written tongue. Eventually he could write full-length poems in Quenya, proving that his invented language had depth and sophistication. Busy with pen and paper and philology, Ronald thrived.

Once he had created Quenya, Ronald hit on another revelation: a language must have people to speak it, people with a history, a heritage, traditions, and stories to tell. So he invented them. Such people he called Elves, and in the coming years he would write their stories. Their language would be named high-Elvish and their land, a place called Middle-earth.

But the reality of the "life of Men," as Ronald called it, changed his world forever. On June 28, 1914, Archduke Franz Ferdinand and his wife were assassinated in far-off Bosnia. Events mushroomed as no one could have imagined, and on August 4, Great Britain and Germany were at war.

Young men poured out of Oxford to become officers in the service of His Majesty King George V. All four T.C.B.S. members served: Rob Gilson, Geoffrey Smith, and Ronald Tolkien in the army; Christopher Wiseman in the Royal Navy.

Ronald, so close to earning his degree at Oxford, postponed active duty and stayed at university. In a best-case plan, he joined the Officers Training Corps at Oxford while finishing his studies and taking a "first," top honors, when he graduated in 1915. Commissioned as an officer into the Lancashire Fusiliers, Ronald wrote to Edith from training camp that November. Though frustrated with army routine, he still had some time for literary pursuits, as he mentioned a poem he'd written.

The usual kind of morning stand about and freezing and then trotting to get warmer so as to freeze again. We ended up by an hour's bomb-throwing with dummies. Lunch and a freezing afternoon. All the hot days of summer we doubled about at full speed and perspiration, now we stand in icy groups in the open being talked at! Tea and another scramble—I fought for a place at the stove

and made a piece of toast on the end of a knife: what days!
I have written out a pencil copy of "Koritrion."

By spring, it seemed that not much had changed.

This miserable drizzling afternoon I have been reading up
old military lecture-notes again:—and getting bored with
them after an hour and a half. I have done some touches
to my nonsense fairy language—to its improvement.

I often long to work at it and don't let myself 'cause
though I love it so it does seem such a mad hobby!

After months of training in England, Ronald discovered and
switched to the signal corps early in 1916, attracted to its styles
and methods of battlefield communications. Second Lieutenant
(pronounced "leftenant" British-style) Tolkien landed in France
in June 1916, leaving behind his new wife. Ronald and Edith had
married in March.

As a signal officer, 11th Battalion, Lancashire Fusiliers,
British Expeditionary Force,
Ronald was tasked with messaging between officers at
the front, where the fighting
was ongoing, and their commanders at battalion headquarters. His job frustrated

John Ronald Reuel Tolkien in
military uniform.
MS.Tolkien photogr. 4, fol.33r,
The Tolkien Trust ©1977, The Bodleian
Libraries, University of Oxford

him at every turn. Telephones could work, of course, but too often the Germans either wiretapped phone lines or simply cut them. Morse code buzzers "leaked" a good 300 yards through the ground, so their signals could be picked up by the enemy. Ronald often had to rely on other forms of communication: flares, signal lamps, mirrors, and even carrier pigeons. Human runners could deliver messages, but they could move only as fast as they could dodge gunfire. In battle, it took eight hours for headquarters to relay orders to the 11th Battalion.

On July 1, 1916, the Allied forces of Great Britain and France attacked Germany north of the Somme River, an 18.5-mile line of fighting at the Western Front northeast of Paris. Both Rob Gilson and Geoffrey Bache Smith went "over the top" and saw combat during that first week of the offensive. (Ronald's unit was held in reserve until the third week.) Twenty thousand Allied men died on the first day as, line by line, they tried to push across no-man's-land to the German stronghold. Despite advance artillery attacks meant to clear their way, waves of barbed wire ensnared the hapless soldiers. Laden with 65 pounds of equipment each, they made easy targets for German machine guns.

Ronald was amazed to connect with his friend Geoffrey, who survived the first days of battle and showed up at Ronald's billet, his quarters in a private residence, after the first wave of attacks. Then came Ronald's turn to go on duty. On Friday, July 14, his unit moved out, threading its way through "communication alleys," pathways to the trenches at the front line. The objective: to take back the bombed-out village of Ovillers, where the Germans had installed a garrison secured by six machine guns. Charles Carrington, a British officer who wrote about the battle many years later, reported that "they were the Prussian Guard again, a crack regiment known as the 'Cockchafers' [nickname for a kind of beetle]. This was a battle fought in summer heat, conditioned by chalk dust, not mud, and, like Hotspur we were 'dry with rage and extreme toil.'" The author knew his readers

Both sides rolled out masses of barbed wire to impede attacking soldiers.
This photo shows American soldiers laying barbed wire later in the war.
Copyright unknown, Courtesy of Harry S. Truman Library and Museum

would recognize "Hotspur" as Sir Henry Percy, a real knight
and famous character in William Shakespeare's plays.

At midnight, the 11th Battalion went over the top and
attacked the garrison. For the first time, John Ronald Reuel
Tolkien saw war with his own eyes. He would later describe
it as "animal horror." The rolling farmland of northern France
lay stripped of everything, stubs of trees and shelled-out rubble
marking where villages once stood. Worse was the smell of
death, days-old swollen bodies of soldiers caught in barbed wire
or spilled into trenches.

The British battled their way uphill toward a German trench
that ran in front of the garrison. They never reached it; a barbed

wire forest and German gunfire stopped them. One officer led his platoon into the firestorm and was cut down. Five more officers were wounded.

Soldiers commonly saw action for several days at a time and then were relieved by fresh troops. Ronald stayed at the front for three days straight—the first two without sleep until he was finally permitted to nap in a dugout. By Sunday evening, July 16, after several attacks and a slew of missed communications, the Brits overcame the Germans, and a white flag of surrender appeared. Ronald's unit was sent back from the line for a rest, and when he got to his billet, a letter waited. It was from Geoffrey Bache Smith.

15 July 1916

My dear John Ronald,
  I saw in the paper this morning that Rob has been killed.
  I am safe but what does that matter?
  Do please stick to me, you and Christopher. I am very tired and most frightfully depressed at this worst of news.
  Now one realizes in despair what the T.C.B.S. really was.
  O my dear John Ronald what ever are we going to do?

Yours ever,
G.B.S.

The next Friday Ronald took on more duties as battalion signal officer, a huge step up in responsibility. A new offensive in the Battle of the Somme followed, and Ronald's unit moved north near Auchonvillers, "Ocean Villas" to his men. Ronald handled messaging between the battalion and headquarters a mile-and-a-half distant, as the Lancashire Fusiliers shoveled dugouts and broadened trenches. Though the Germans fired on them from time to time, there was no attack, and by August 7

Ronald was dispatched to organize new battalion headquarters farther north. The others of his unit followed, again digging into the war-scarred ground to prepare it for future battle.

By August 10, they had earned a rest and withdrew to a village undamaged by war.

The Battle of the Somme dragged on into September, then October, and then it began to rain. Ronald took ill; he had all the signs of pyrexia, what his men called "trench fever." He'd caught it from a louse, a common result of living in a wet ditch. Thousands of British soldiers were "lousy" with lice. Sick with the high fevers, chills, sweats, and aches of this flu-like illness, Ronald was sent to a hospital far from the line to recover.

But he didn't recover, so in November he was put aboard a ship and sent home to England. He regained enough strength to spend Christmas with Edith. A few days later, Ronald received another blow: Geoffrey Bache Smith had been wounded in an explosion and died of gangrene. Two of the four T.B.C.S. were gone.

The First Battle of the Somme was to drag on for four and a half months until the snow flew in November. By the time the battle ended and opponents dug into their trenches for the winter, the dead and wounded on both sides totaled more than 1.2 million. The Allies had pushed forward only five miles.

Ronald never saw another battle. The symptoms of trench fever came and went; just when he felt recovered enough to return to France, he'd relapse and end up back in the hospital. He made good use of these extended stretches of enforced rest. At the urging of his sole remaining T.C.B.S. mate, Christopher Wiseman, he embarked on writing the first of his great tales, *The Silmarillion*, early in 1917. He kept at his writing, even as he moved back and forth among various army posts in England, military hospitals, and home with Edith.

Ronald Tolkien never thought of himself as much of a soldier. In World War II he wrote to his son Michael, then a military cadet, reflecting on his own experiences two decades before. "I suffered once what you are going through, if rather differently: because I was very inefficient and unmilitary (and we are alike only in sharing a deep sympathy and feeling for the 'tommy,' especially the plain soldier from the agricultural counties.)"

Tolkien far more respected the common soldier than he did his fellow officers, and he styled his Hobbit-hero Sam Gamgee after the batmen he met, the lower-class Englishmen who served a dual role as soldiers and personal assistants to British officers. "My 'Samwise' is indeed . . . largely a reflexion of the English soldier—grafted on the village-boys of early days, the memory of the privates and my batmen that I knew in the 1914 War, and recognized as so far superior to myself."

When the war ended in November 1918, Ronald took a job with the New English Dictionary (now called the Oxford English Dictionary) and then won his first teaching job at the University of Leeds, where he quickly earned a professorship in 1924. He stayed only briefly; Oxford offered him a position as professor of Anglo-Saxon, and off he went with Edith and their two sons. (They later added a third son and a daughter.)

Teaching, as well as his academic research in Early and Middle English on sagas like *Beowulf* and *Sir Gawain and the Green Knight*, plus his own writing, all ate up Ronald's time in the coming years as his family grew and they moved to ever-better homes. In the summer of 1930 he began *The Hobbit*, which appeared in print seven years later. His publisher asked for a sequel, and Ronald began a new project in the fall of 1937, which morphed into a series he called *The Lord of the Rings*, the saga of Dwarves, Elves, Hobbits, and Men who battle a great evil to save their way of life.

J. R. R. Tolkien began writing *The Lord of the Rings* as the rising menace of Nazi Germany drew England into World War II. His masterpiece—three books in all—didn't appear in print until the mid-1950s. The series became wildly popular in the

1960s with youth in North America and Europe; its themes of good versus evil and environmental responsibility appealed to them, especially in the context of America's conduct in the Vietnam War.

Legions of historians and literary critics would examine John Ronald Reuel Tolkien's stories in the years to come. Some of them drew very specific conclusions—that, for example, the author imagined his Hobbits as England's foot soldiers, the Orcs as Germans, or metal monsters as tanks. Would Ronald have agreed? Most likely not.

He long denied that his stories were allegories or symbols of the Great War and the Second World War that followed. Certainly, though, war's sounds, smells, and monumental visuals lodged in his brain. He could not escape his memories, and he didn't try to deny them. Neither did he dwell on them. They were simply *there*, a rich stock of impressions that appeared as themes in his tales—the battle of good against evil, the destruction of the land, courage in the face of death, the horror of mechanized warfare, the need for a circle of friends, the fellowship of those fighting for a common cause, the nobility of sacrificing oneself for another.

When he prepared for a second edition of the books in the mid-1960s, J. R. R. Tolkien shared his thoughts in a new foreword. Now almost 75, he had the wisdom and perspective of a life long lived as he looked back on his soldier years. It must have seemed that the world had forgotten its first Great War as well as the Second World War that followed:

One has indeed personally to come under the shadow of war to feel fully its oppression; but as the years go by it seems now often forgotten that to be caught in youth by 1914 was no less hideous an experience than to be involved in 1939 and the following years. By 1918 all but one of my close friends were dead.

★ ★ ★

SHELL SHOCK—A WOUND OF WAR

In every war, soldiers are wounded not just in body but in mind. Thousands returned from the Great War with mental illness. The worst cases lived out their days in hospitals, silent shells of men unable to communicate. The rest came home to their families. Today we call such mental illness PTSD— post-traumatic stress disorder. To soldiers then, the term was shell shock—men left weeping or dazed, some with gaping mouths and unfocused eyes, some with diarrhea, others with night terrors or uncontrollable anxiety.

Shell shock afflicted soldiers of all nations and ranks, including an ordinary Australian named Edward Noel Denovan. Denovan, an electric lineman, left his family to serve as a gunner in the Australia Field Artillery in France. Noel's Casualty Report detailed every illness and injury he suffered. He was hospitalized often, once for taking a bullet in his knee during the Battle of Arras in April 1917. A severe ear infection led to his early discharge from the army.

However, the record never showed Noel's troubled mental state. When he returned home, his family realized he was not the same man. But the change in Noel's psychological state wasn't talked about. In those days, families didn't discuss unpleasant matters like cancer or depression. Noel

continued on the next page . . .

★ ★ ★

★ ★ ★

Australian gunner Noel Denovan poses for his military portrait before leaving for France.
Courtesy of Michelle Denovan

himself did not speak of his war experiences.

Noel abandoned his family, and his jobless wife raised their five children with government aid. During World War II, he returned to military duty near Sydney. Still, it seems he never shared his wartime memories—painful or otherwise—and he took them to his grave.

★ ★ ★

THE STUDENT

***

WALTER KOESSLER

Walter Koessler (1891–1966?) was born in the German city of Strasbourg in Alsace-Lorraine, a strip of territory that Germany and France had fought over for decades. Walter was studying architecture at the university in Karlsruhe in 1914 when Germany and France again went to war. The first devastating battles made it clear that Germany wouldn't win a quick victory, and the German army called up students like Walter to serve in its officer corps. Walter brought a camera along, and years later, he arranged his photos into an album he titled "Walter Koessler 1914–1918."

In 2011, nearly 100 years after Germany joined Austria-Hungary to fight the Allies in World War I, a recent college graduate named Dean Putney was getting ready to go back to California after Thanksgiving at his parents' home in Maine. His mother handed him something he'd never seen, an old album passed down through the years. It was the work of Walter Koessler, his great-grandfather on his mother's side, a man Dean had never met.

Dean's mother had handed him a treasure—a record of Walter Koessler's daily life as an officer in the German army. Its 107 pages are filled with 670 photographs, plus typewritten notes and sketches. Putney decided to publish the album privately and used Kickstarter to crowdsource the funding he needed to see the project through.

The result is a masterpiece. To thumb through the pages of Walter Koessler's album is to see war close up through the eyes of a young man who was a German officer. Day by day, from 1914 well into 1918, Walter lived through and bore witness to the war with his camera.

It's often said that a picture is worth a thousand words. Walter Koessler's remarkable images are worth volumes.

This photo was taken during Walter's first months as a German officer. He poses with his motorbike. *Dean Putney*

Time-out for a haircut in the woods. Most men in the trench at the back wear the *Pickelhaube*, the spiked helmet of the German soldier. *Dean Putney*

Walter served as an artillery officer in the German army's 10th Artillery Reserve Battalion. Many photos show German cannons, some camouflaged with trees. This one shows artillerymen straddling the barrel of their cannon. *Dean Putney*

Livestock troughs serve as a spot to freshen up and perhaps do some laundry. *Dean Putney*

Throughout a good part of 1915, Walter's unit spent time in the trenches in France, probably near Bourg Bruche in Alsace. His photos show how solidly the Germans built their trenches, quite the contrast from the poorly constructed Allied trenches across no-man's-land (the wasteland between the two armies). Barbed wire and clear-cut forests dominate many of his pictures. He also provided a written account of a patrol he led, along with a sketch showing his path through enemy territory.

With an architect's eye, Walter captures images of German trenches in various stages of construction and then in use.

Dean Putney

Soldiers play cards when sunlight falls on a trench. A tidy garden has been planted, as well. *Dean Putney*

All through World War I, Walter shot scores of candid photos of other soldiers—officers and ordinary infantrymen—at work and during their time off. Only a few were marked with names.

This picture is probably from 1915, and the solider seems to be quite young. By the end of the war, Germany had lost two million men, and boys as young as 16 were being drafted. *Dean Putney*

Walter's album traces the passing of time from warm seasons to cold and over again, well into 1918. Over that time, Walter served on both the Western and Eastern Fronts. His album holds pictures of local people, their families, and their villages. He also snapped shots of a visit from Kaiser Wilhelm II to Strasbourg, which coincided with Walter's leave to visit his family in 1917.

As the war progressed, Walter took far more pictures showing destruction, including a train derailment, bombed-out buildings, and photos of comrades killed in battle, with blankets covering their heads and torsos.

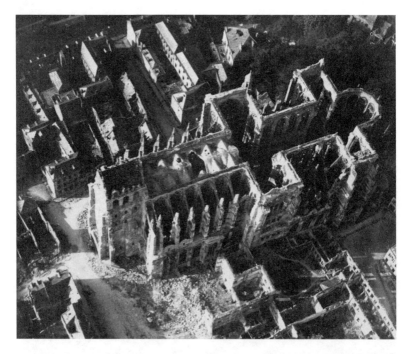

Walter's photos of churches in ruins contrast starkly with his other images of tranquil towns and smiling villagers. In 1917, Walter flew in a German aircraft to make a photographic record of the French village of Saint-Quentin, especially its bombed-out cathedral. Neither the Germans nor the French would admit they had fired on it. *Dean Putney*

Tanks were known as "mobile crematoriums" because if shell fire hit them, their occupants would burn to death. This picture was taken in 1917.
Dean Putney

The final photos in Walter's album show soldiers packing cannons to transport them home from the war. Walter himself returned to Strasbourg. The family lore says Walter had political differences with the city fathers. In 1924, Walter, his first wife Kathrin, and their son Wolfgang (Dean Putney's grandfather) emigrated from Alsace to Los Angeles. Walter worked as a set designer for movies and TV.

Walter's family believed he did set design for the 1930 film *All Quiet on the Western Front*, a classic movie drawn from a book written by another German soldier, Erich Maria Remarque.

THE AVIATRIX

* * *

KATHERINE STINSON

> *The unflappable Katherine Stinson (1891–1977), one of America's premier pilots, had thrilled crowds and made headlines in the United States and Canada when she asked the US War Department for a flying job in the Great War.*

In the summer of 1928, a newspaper reporter from California stopped by the home of a New Mexico state official to speak with his wife. She was busy mending a broken screen, and the reporter remarked how different it was for her to be keeping house than working the job she'd held 10 years earlier.

Not really, Katherine Stinson Otero replied. "As an aviator I often spent hours at a time working on the fabric of my airplane wings after they had been damaged in forced landings or otherwise. I think my early training prepared me for my present duties."

It was a modest comment from a modest woman who 15 years before had been the darling of the nation, America's "Flying Schoolgirl."

In the spring of 1912, Katherine Stinson flew a series of maneuvers at Cicero Field in Chicago to become only the fourth American woman to earn a pilot's license. The concept of a female flyer was so new that the papers hadn't settled on a term for a woman pilot until the word *aviatrix* appeared.

> "I enjoy flying," said Miss Stinson when she reached the earth, "but I am not in it for the fun of it. I intend continuing my musical education in Europe. Girl aviators are a novelty now, and I believe I can make more money in quicker time with an aeroplane than in any other business."

Unflappable. That was Katherine Stinson. How else could one explain a young woman who took up flying so she could sail to Europe and study piano?

But flying eventually trumped piano lessons, and within months Katherine Stinson became one of the nation's leading barnstormers—pilots who traveled from town to town performing daring feats of acrobatic flying to adoring crowds. She traveled by railroad, dismantling her fabric-winged biplane between performances, packing it into shipping crates, and taking it with her on the train. Her performances earned her top dollar, anywhere from $1,000 to $2,000 or more a week, when the average American brought home just $700 a year.

As thrilling and lucrative as the flying was, it was dangerous, and many a crowd witnessed deadly crashes as barnstormers miscalculated their dives, rolls, loops, and upside-down flight. Other times, a plane's motor would simply quit, and pilots would try to glide their aircraft down to a safe landing. They didn't always succeed.

The inherent dangers of barnstorming seemed to have little impact on Katherine. She paid very close attention to maintaining her planes and hired the best mechanicians, as they were then called, to keep them airworthy. She seemed to be self-confident, unworried about the risks she took. Once she recovered an 80-horsepower airplane motor from a crash that killed its pilot, the flamboyant Lincoln Beachey, and then used it in her own custom-built plane. Perhaps Katherine, like so many her age, couldn't envision herself dying. But more likely, she didn't worry because she was careful, calm, and very well-prepared.

In 1913 "Katie" Stinson first took her show on the road to Cincinnati, where the *Cincinnati Enquirer* reported that "the little Southern girl who has been driving a Wright bi-plane . . . experienced her first fall." She was the afternoon's entertainment for a national gathering of members of the Moose Club and was climbing skyward when the crowd could see she had problems with the motor.

> The little aviatrice, although the engine stalled, managed the machine with marvelous skill and guided it in its fall to a soft field, where it landed head-on. . . .
>
> The flight was made just as the Moose were enjoying a burgoo feast [a stew made famous at the Kentucky Derby], and for a while it cast a gloom over the gathering. But when the little bird-girl emerged from the distant cornfield there was a shout of joy that could be heard a mile away.

In 1915, Katie returned to Cicero Field to become the first woman to complete a loop, flying her plane in the same circular fashion that we use to write a cursive *e*. On the West Coast, she took to the air at night, each wingtip decked out with a burning flare, as she used her plane like a pen to trace the letters *C-A-L* in the darkness.

It seemed there was nothing Katherine Stinson wouldn't try with an airplane. In 1916 she took her biplane with her on an ocean liner and sailed to Asia, where she amazed crowds in

China and Japan. Later that year, the *Enquirer* predicted certain death for this young woman, "the only one of her sex to loop the loop" and "the first aviator to flirt with death in the air at night." At five feet five inches and a bit over 100 pounds, it took strong muscles for Katherine to manage a flying machine that wasn't equipped with powered controls.

Her sister and brothers also went into flying, and the Stinsons formed a flight training school near San Antonio, Texas. Marjorie, her next younger sibling, earned the title of "Flying Schoolmarm" by training more than 100 student pilots. Their brothers Eddie and Jack also shared the family passion for planes. Years later, Eddie, also a stunt pilot, went on to establish the Stinson Aircraft Company. He died in a crash in 1932.

When Canada went to war against Germany in 1914, pilots were in high demand to fly for the Allies, and young Canadians arrived in San Antonio to be trained at the Stinsons' flight school. The very first American flyers, members of the US 1st Aero Squadron, showed up there as well. In fact, the maneuvers Katherine performed in her shows were the same ones army pilots used to dodge enemy bullets in aerial dogfights against the Germans. More than likely she had taught them her techniques.

America's "Flying Schoolgirl,"
Katherine Stinson.
Library of Congress, LC-B2-4142-5

How ironic it was when these new pilots joined their squadrons in Europe, while their instructors, Katherine and Marjorie Stinson, were denied the same chance. Twice Katherine applied to the American Expeditionary Force (AEF) Air Service to work as a pilot, and twice the top brass in the army—and the secretary of war—said no. For a woman to fly for the army was unthinkable.

In 1918 Katherine signed on as an employee of the US Post Office and was among the first pilots to fly airmail. She made yet another headline in May 1918 when she set a record, flying 783 miles in 10 hours from Chicago to New York. Bad weather forced her to land near Binghamton, New York, as *Aerial Age Weekly* reported:

> Katherine Stinson, who left Chicago on the morning of May 23 with Government mail for New York, landed two miles north of Binghamton at 6:50 this evening. She met with an accident while attempting a landing, the machine turning turtle just as it reached the ground. The propeller was smashed and one of the wings damaged. Miss Stinson was uninjured.

Katherine made another splash in Alberta, Canada, that July when she piloted the first airmail flight in western Canada, from Calgary to Edmonton.

The army might have forbidden her to fly in France, but the US government knew that a flying schoolgirl could appeal to Americans' hearts and open their pocketbooks. Put to work as an airborne publicity stunt, Katherine flew from town to town on a campaign to sell Liberty Bonds to help pay for the war. She also raised $2 million for the American Red Cross, and she ended that fundraising journey by landing on a white cross in front of the Washington Monument.

Katherine may have impressed the government and the Red Cross by making millions for them, but in her own heart she

A poster features Katherine Stinson's success in flying the first airmail in western Canada in 1918. *City of Edmonton Archives*

Women ambulance drivers follow military protocol as they serve in the Red Cross. *Library of Congress, LC-DIG-ds-01290*

yearned to get to France. If she couldn't fly for the war effort, she certainly could drive, so when the Red Cross advertised for 300 women to join the ambulance corps in August 1918, she signed up. Katherine set sail for France, where she learned how to maneuver a Ford ambulance manufactured at home in Detroit. Many years later, she recalled her experience: "I learned to drive a Ford car in the streets of Paris, being taught to [drive] by French taxi drivers in French, and I didn't know any French, and they—I would get into the wrong lane and they didn't like it one little bit."

The next time Americans read about Katherine was when she came home. One of 2,300 passengers on the USS *Harrisburg*, a troopship loaded with soldiers, sailors, and Red Cross workers, Katherine was interviewed when the ship docked in New York.

She explained that after the war, she'd finally gotten permission to work as a pilot and was all set to fly mail between Paris and General Pershing's army headquarters when she "contracted a heavy cold while driving an ambulance. She said she hoped her next airplane flight would be one across the Atlantic."

Like so many others in 1918, Katherine had taken ill. She ended up in the hospital in Paris, so sick with influenza that she couldn't fly at all. Instead, she came home, and the deadly flu virus was followed by a serious case of tuberculosis. It took a long time for her to recover. She spent years in sanitoriums for patients like her, first in New York and then in Santa Fe, New Mexico, where the sunny, dry climate was thought to benefit people with lung disease. There she met another pilot, a young man named Miguel Otero who'd flown in France during the Great War. They married in 1927, and Katherine developed another set of skills as an architect. She and Miguel also raised her four nieces and nephews.

In 1960, when researchers compiled a list of interviews for an aviation project for *American Heritage Magazine*, Katherine's name made the list. Long forgotten as a pioneer in American aviation, she sat with Miguel for a tape-recorded interview. Clearly, by this time, Katherine's mind was starting to fade, and in the course of the interview, Miguel stepped in several times to gently nudge his wife's failing memory. This interview was probably one of the last times Katherine spoke of her days as a pilot and her life during World War I. She spent her later years in poor health and died in 1977.

THE FAMILY

✱ ✱ ✱

THE YOUNG ROOSEVELTS

> *When Theodore Roosevelt (1858–1919) became president of the United States in 1901, he moved his large family into the White House, where they lived until 1909. At four o'clock in the afternoon most days, the president stopped work to romp with his children and their pets. Little did he know that his children, when grown, would take part in the Great War.*

In April 1914 a famous American and his son went missing in the Amazon jungle. They were America's 26th president, Theodore Roosevelt, and his son Kermit Roosevelt, age 24. At 55, an old man by the standards of his day and with nothing better to do, Theodore, and his son, had joined a Brazilian explorer named Candida Rendon and a small party of scientists and adventurers. Rendon had spotted the headwaters of a stream, and he suspected that a thousand kilometers north or more, its murky waters would swell into a tributary of the mighty Amazon River. Kermit, newly graduated from Harvard College and working at his first job in Brazil, joined in building dugout canoes to carry the party down the unmapped river. The adventure offered the former president his "last chance to be a boy," and off they went. Six weeks later, no one had heard a word from them.

They almost died. Five of the dugouts were lost in swirling rapids as the stream grew into a raging river, and one boatman drowned. A second boatman murdered a third, and the others abandoned the guilty man to the justice of the jungle, knowing that the Indians who stalked them were sure to kill him with one of their poison-tipped arrows.

Theodore gashed his leg, opening up an old wound that became infected. Mosquitoes stung him and he contracted malaria, his fever rising to 105 degrees and his body dehydrating from diarrhea. The sick man told his son and the others to leave him behind to die. A veteran outdoorsman, Theodore carried a tiny glass vial filled with poison. One crush of the vial with his teeth, and his agony would end.

A product of a strong Victorian upbringing, Theodore believed it was his responsibility to sacrifice himself so that others might live. Such was the duty of a man in 1914.

But with duty came honor, as Kermit understood his role as a son. "Honor thy father," the fifth commandment ordered, and Kermit did. He refused to abandon his father and insisted he continue the journey with the explorers. When they picked up their loaded dugouts to carry them around treacherous points along the river, Kermit helped his father to hobble and rest, hobble and rest.

Father and son survived their ordeal, and, 600 miles from where they had started their voyage down the Rio da Dúvida ("River of Doubt"), they emerged from the jungle. In honor of the courageous survivor, the river was given a new name: Rio Roosevelt.

Duty, honor, and sacrifice. Kermit and the other Roosevelts grew up learning to follow these virtues. It was the duty of a man to be a loving husband and father whose hard work put food on the table and a roof over his children's heads. It was the duty of a woman to honor her husband as she created a loving home, a refuge from the dirty streets and dirty business of American commerce and industry. It was a child's duty to obey his or her parents, work hard at lessons, and go to Sunday school.

If war came, a young man was expected to serve his country and perhaps sacrifice his life. Theodore and Edith Roosevelt would have expected nothing less. The well-off Roosevelts, born to wealth yet taught to serve others, had long lived with a second code of honor: work hard, play hard, and protect others whose lives were less fortunate than theirs.

As expected of couples in their social class, Theodore and Edith Roosevelt had done their duty and raised a large family at Sagamore Hill, their rambling home on Long Island, New York. They had six children: Alice, Ted, Kermit, Ethel, Archie, and Quentin. Alice, the eldest, was the daughter of Theodore and his first wife, Alice Lee Roosevelt, who died after Alice was born.

Though devoted to her siblings and father, Alice broke every rule she could and was something of a brat. Ted, first child of Theodore and his second wife, Edith, tried to follow his larger-than-life father as best he could. Kermit, the boy who liked to travel with his father, came next, followed by Ethel, the family's middle child, her father's "jolly naughty whacky baby." Archibald—Archie for short—could be awkward with others but adored Quentin, the youngest of the family. Quentin had a national reputation. He'd once smuggled a pony up the White House elevator to pay a visit to Archie, who was sick in bed.

Two months after Kermit and Theodore Roosevelt returned from South America, Europe exploded. With the June 28, 1914, assassination of Archduke Franz Ferdinand, all of Europe took sides and made declarations of war.

On August 4, showing an appalling lack of honor, Germany invaded neutral Belgium, looking to roll through the small

The family of Theodore Roosevelt poses for a portrait in 1903. Pictured (l. to r.) are Quentin, Theodore, Ted, Archie, Alice, Kermit, Edith, and Ethel. *Library of Congress, LC-USZ62-113665*

country and attack France from the north. Germany's well-trained soldiers leveled villages, burned fields, and sent millions of people running for their lives. The German army killed some 5,400 Belgian and French civilians, many if not most in massacres and executions, in the first two months of war.

Theodore Roosevelt closely followed the march of events and began to write a book about the conflict in Europe. His words lit up the facts—"hell yawned" and "volcanoes gleamed." One minute, Europeans were going about their daily lives, busy with work and play. Then, like the unsuspecting passengers on the *Titanic*, "in one shattering moment, death smote the floating host."

Theodore wondered whether the disaster would engulf his own children, who were busy building their lives. Except for Quentin, all the young Roosevelts were married. The boys, now young men, were running businesses and starting families. Ethel had a baby to care for, and Alice lived in Washington as a congressman's wife.

Convinced that his sons would be called upon to fight the German menace, the former president also realized that his country was not prepared. He'd seen war for himself. In 1898, Theodore had left his wife and children to drive the Spanish out of Cuba in the Spanish-American War. He had returned home a hero, the courageous Colonel Roosevelt who had led the US 1st Volunteer Cavalry, the Rough Riders, in the famous charge up San Juan Hill.

As it happened, a Roosevelt daughter got to the war in Europe before any of her brothers. In September 1914, Ethel sailed for France with her husband, Dick Derby, a surgeon, to work at an American hospital in Paris. Ethel left her own baby boy with her parents to do her part in France. Married just a year and a half, Ethel was excited to think she and Dick would learn French together and see a bit of Europe.

When Ethel and Dick arrived in Paris, their hospital visits horrified them. Dick was dismayed to see how wounded soldiers were carried from the Western Front all the way to Paris on trains. In the chaos, some had endured a week or more on crowded railway cars meant for transporting ammunition to the front. Deaths from bacterial infections were staggering.

Though she was not trained for nursing, Ethel worked alongside Dick doing what she could. She transported patients for X-rays, changed dirty bandages, made splints to support injured limbs, and kept company with gravely wounded British soldiers.

Some had had their legs blown off, and Ethel fretted about how to find the cash to pay for artificial limbs. She took things hard. "I don't go much in the wards because I cannot bear it," she wrote home. "Such appalling wounds. . . . Nearly everything is infected."

In these days before antibiotics were discovered, many wounded young men died from infection. Once a soldier was hit by a bullet or shell fragments, doctors had only a 12-hour window of opportunity to prevent bacteria from invading his body. The solution for combating infection, Dick came to realize, was to treat a wounded soldier as close to the front as possible and then transport him by ambulance to a field hospital. Treatment at the front and a strong corps of ambulance drivers to take injured men to field hospitals—these could make the difference between life and death. Eventually the French army would figure that out, but for many of these raw young soldiers in September 1914, it was too late.

Ethel and Dick returned home that winter to find that most Americans were not thinking about the war. President Woodrow Wilson had declared that the United States would stay officially neutral and not take sides. In 1915, Wilson accepted Germany's apology after German U-boats torpedoed the *Lusitania*, a British passenger ship, killing 128 Americans among nearly 2,000 civilians. Still safe at home, most Americans felt Europe's problems had little to do with them.

But not the Roosevelts. In the summers of 1915 and '16, Ethel's brothers and her husband went to a camp in Plattsburgh, New York, for a month of military training unauthorized by the army. Mostly businessmen and students from Harvard, Yale, and Princeton, these Ivy Leaguers planned to be ready if war came to the United States. They drilled, sometimes with broomsticks because rifles were in short supply. They studied the art of war, its strategy and tactics, as spelled out in their training manuals. President Wilson might be in denial about the dangers of Germany, but they were not. When the time came, the Roosevelt men would be ready. It was a matter of duty, honor, and sacrifice.

Fed up with Wilson's stand on neutrality, Kermit Roosevelt decided to wait no longer and joined the British Army in 1917. Leaving his wife, Belle, and their new son, he was commissioned an officer and left for far-off Mesopotamia, where Britain was fighting the Ottoman Empire. When Kermit left, isolationism still dominated American foreign policy. President Wilson campaigned for reelection on the slogan "He kept us out of war," and Americans returned him to the White House later that year.

At Sagamore Hill, Theodore Roosevelt waited like a lion sniffing the wind for trouble. In the winter of 1917, trouble came. First the British intercepted a German telegram sent to the Mexican government saying that if Mexico agreed to harbor German U-boats, Germany would support Mexico in a war to reclaim Arizona, New Mexico, and Texas from the United States. Then Germany announced on February 1 that it would no longer restrict submarine warfare and would attack any type of ship, whether military, merchant, or passenger vessel. But in March, when German U-boats sank three American merchant ships filled with cargo, Woodrow Wilson's mood finally changed.

Early in April 1917, the United States declared war on Germany and Austria-Hungary. The Roosevelts mobilized. Theodore wrote a personal letter to General John Pershing requesting assignments for Ted and Archie—nothing exceptional, their father pointedly asked, just a chance to get to France as fast as possible with the American Expeditionary Forces (AEF). Theodore himself had every intention of serving as well, and he called at the White House to ask the president's permission to raise a division of soldiers. President Wilson, long antagonized by Theodore Roosevelt's criticism of his presidency, coldly denied his request, an embarrassment to the old Rough Rider.

With Kermit already in the Middle East, the other Roosevelts waited for the call to duty. Then their orders came through. On June 20, Ted and Archie left for France to serve under Pershing. Thanks to their training at summer camp, both held commissions as officers. Not to be outdone, Ted's wife, Eleanor (not cousin Eleanor who married a distant Roosevelt relative named Franklin), jumped at the chance to work in Paris for the YMCA.

That left Quentin. Like his Harvard classmates, he dropped out of college to get in on the action. Always the daredevil, Quentin already had crashed his motorcycle into a tree near home. Now he looked skyward and applied for pilot training.

Quentin had a bad back and was nearsighted to boot, but he squeaked through his army physical and memorized the eye chart before his exam. He took to flying like a bird to the air, practicing his maneuvers over Sagamore Hill where his father could watch. In July 1917, 19-year-old Lieutenant Quentin Roosevelt packed his trunk to sail for France. Like so many young men that summer, he left the love of his life behind. She was Flora Payne Whitney, a sweet, quiet girl and heiress to two family fortunes.

Theodore and Edith Roosevelt knew that Quentin had asked Flora to marry him and that the young couple was secretly engaged. But nothing was said about it as her parents and his went to the docks in Manhattan to kiss him good-bye. Alice, who also showed up to bid her youngest brother farewell, was heard to say that her father assumed he would lose a son in battle.

By summer's end in 1917, with three years of fighting and millions of lives lost, the line of battle between the Allies and Germany had moved nowhere. Both sides were dug into trenches that snaked from the French coast inland for hundreds of miles. The Great War had become a war of attrition, a matter of seeing which side could outlast its enemy.

As winter came, Russia, turned upside down by the Bolshevik Revolution, dropped out of the war. Germany transferred 570,000 troops from the Eastern Front to the Western Front, and its brilliant General Eric Ludendorff made plans for a spring offensive in France. From all appearances, the Allies were losing their grip. British and French soldiers were tired and beaten up. Duty, honor, and sacrifice—such ideals seemed absurd amid the mud and barbed wire along the Western Front.

Then fortune began to change. The first wave of American soldiers with the American Expeditionary Forces arrived at the front with Ted and Archie Roosevelt among them. Both brothers wore a 1 on their sleeves—the insignia of the US Army's First Division, the Big Red One. Each held a command, Ted as a major and Archie as a captain. Ethel's husband, Dr. Dick Derby, was back in France as well, doing surgery in a field hospital. It was March 1918, the fourth time spring had come since the Great War began.

The warring sides returned to battle. The Germans knew that the full flush of American troops would arrive in France by summer. Now was their chance to break through the Western Front for good. General Ludendorff designed a three-stage battle plan. In the first move of his "shock and awe" campaign, his best troops would charge across the trenches under the cover of smoke shells and poison gas. A second wave of light artillery would engage Allied soldiers as they returned fire from their machine gun nests. The third wave, an all-out assault of firepower, would overwhelm the entrenched Allied soldiers as the superior German infantry stormed across the battlefields, killing everyone and obliterating everything in its way.

The campaign began on March 21, when the Germans struck in five offensives along the Western Front. At first, Ludendorff's plan seemed brilliant. In 40 days, the German army pushed forward 40 miles and took 70,000 Allied soldiers as prisoners. Another 200,000 Allied soldiers were taken out of action, wounded or killed.

Among the wounded was Captain Archie Roosevelt. Just as Ludendorff's offensive began, Archie was shot in both his

Dick Derby, Archie Roosevelt, Eleanor Butler Roosevelt, and Kermit
Roosevelt sit for a portrait in 1918.
Library of Congress, LC-USZ62-135060

arm and leg. By now, the army's medical men had learned the
grim lessons of 1914, and Archie was treated right at the front.
Once his condition was stable, an ambulance took him from the
trenches to a field hospital, where doctors peeled away the cov-
erings to his wounds. Archie's knees had taken shrapnel, and his

arm was shattered in two places. He would need more surgery, but he would eventually get well.

Archie faced a long, uncomfortable stay in the hospital, his left arm hanging in traction straight out from his body. But then he got a piece of happy news: his brother-in-law Dick Derby arrived for a visit with a letter from Ethel in hand. Ethel had written Dick that Archie had a son—Archibald Roosevelt Junior. Of course, Archie's wife Grace had written to him as well, but none of her letters had made it across the ocean to France.

When a telegram about Archie's injuries reached Sagamore Hill, his proud—and relieved—father wrote back that he was a "hero in the family." Theodore went on to describe the scene when he and Edith got the news. They had dinner guests, and Edith, not usually given to public displays of emotion, ordered a servant to bring a bottle of wine.

> [A]ll four of us filled the glasses and drank them off to you; then Mother, her eyes shining, her cheeks flushed, as pretty as a picture, and as spirited as any heroine of romance, dashed her glass on the floor, shivering it in pieces, saying "That glass shall never be drunk out of again"; and the rest of us followed suit and broke our glasses too.

As Archie began to recover, doctors discovered that his injuries were far graver than they had thought. He would get better, they told him, but he was medically unfit to fight. Officially, Archie was out of the Big Red One. When he limped off a troopship in New York later that year, Archie's chest was decorated with medals. One was the French Croix de Guerre, awarded to Archie in his hospital bed by a French general with a kiss on each cheek.

Germany continued to launch fresh offensives against the Allies. In April the Germans struck in Flanders, the northern part of Belgium that had seen so much fighting in the war's opening months. In May the Germans made another assault in northeast France over a rocky ridge with the unlikely name *Chemin des Dames*, the "Road of the Ladies." Three days later, the Germans had battled their way to the town of Château-Thierry. Paris was only 50 miles away.

It came time for the AEF to show its stuff, and the First Division seemed to be the best prepared for the challenge. On May 28, 1918, company commander Theodore Roosevelt Jr. received orders to take a German observation point that sat inside the small French village of Cantigny. Ted wasn't one to stand aside and let others take risks he wouldn't take himself. With the support of French airplanes overhead, Ted and his men attacked and took the village. They used rifles, machine guns, and bayonets against the Germans, who had orders to fight to the death.

The Germans retaliated in a fierce bombardment, showering the Americans with artillery. For two days, shells filled

with explosives and poison gas rained down on the Americans. Clouds of noxious vapor hung close to the ground and caught Ted and others by surprise. It was too late for their gas masks to be of much use.

Eleanor Butler Roosevelt and her husband, Ted, posed for this photo two days after the war ended. Eleanor wears the YMCA uniform she designed for her work in France. Ted uses a cane, as the war left him with a limp.
McCormick Research Center

Despite damage to his lungs and a temporary blindness, Ted refused to go to the hospital. He had men to command, men who were not giving up the ground they'd won from the Germans. The Battle of Cantigny took its toll; Ted was one of the 1,000 Americans killed or wounded. But the Americans held on to Cantigny, and when Ted's general made his report to headquarters, he cited Ted for conspicuous gallantry in action.

Far from the action, at a French air base, Quentin was training as a Chasse (pursuit) pilot. His mission: to bring down enemy planes. Far more mechanical than his brothers, Quentin enjoyed the process of learning to fly his plane and shoot at the same time. "From what I can gather about half the game in 'chasse' is good machine gun work," he wrote in a letter home. In the next, Quentin shared more about his training.

> First there are no guns on the planes and you have to go up a couple of thousand metres, drop over a paper parachute, and then chase it, manoevring round it. After that you start [shooting], beginning on fixed balloons and ending with a sleeve towed by another plane. In all that work they keep record of your shots, and count the hits afterward.

Quentin made friends easily and was well liked by his fellow pilots. Off duty the airmen swapped stories and shared bottles of champagne. More experienced pilots warned Quentin not to take risks when he flew. Quentin shared their anger after American officials cut their flight pay, and he griped in a letter about the way headquarters handed out awards to pilots and their ground crews.

> [T]he new service stripe regulations came out, and we got it in the neck again. In the aviation section one has to be six months in actual combat at the front to get a

stripe; that means that a mechanic working near the front and bombarded every night has nothing to distinguish him from the Washington embusqué [someone working a desk job to escape the fighting]. A pilot has to last six months and they hardly ever keep a chasse pilot up more than three. Also some one like Ham Coolidge [Quentin's Harvard classmate] for instance, who is testing planes back at the school and doing dangerous work gets no credit and yet we kill on an average of one a week at the school.

So far from the action, Quentin ached to fly with a British or French air unit as soon as he could. But at Christmastime he caught pneumonia, which kept him sick in bed and sick at heart. For a time, restless and blue, he stopped writing letters home, which worried his mother and annoyed his father. Quentin was equally frustrated about waiting to marry Flora, and though she had applied for permission to come to France for a wedding, her request was denied. The army had tightened up on letting wives and fiancées into France. The only American women getting to Paris were nurses, telephone operators, entertainers, and volunteers for the Red Cross, YMCA, and Salvation Army.

Now and again Quentin got leave and rode his motorcycle to visit his sister-in-law Eleanor in Paris, where she worked for the YMCA. Eleanor had the gift of hospitality and a knack for homemaking, and she was delighted to be one of the lucky American wives who had managed to get to the war. She opened her house in Paris to a number of visiting American officers, including all three of the Roosevelt brothers and Ethel's husband, Dick. Her French neighbors gossiped about the *Américaine* who they suspected was running a brothel.

At long last Quentin got his orders to report for duty, not to a French or British squadron as he'd expected, but to the 95th Aero Squadron, 1st Pursuit Group of the brand-new US

Army Air Service. The new group was assigned to the Château-Thierry sector northeast of Paris. The French town was still in German hands, but the air above was fair game for pilots. They flew Nieuports, one-man bi-wing planes that Quentin thought were tricky to handle. The numbers were not in his favor. A chasse pilot lived an average of 11 days when Quentin arrived at the Western Front.

In mid-July 1918, just after Quentin's arrival at the front, the Germans launched yet another offensive at Château-Thierry in what came to be called the Second Battle of the Marne. A few days later, Quentin wrote home to say he believed he had shot down a German fighter, his first victory.

Pilots tended to have a dark humor and talked among themselves about the prospect of dying and how it would feel to be shot down. Quentin tried to prepare his family for the worst. "There's no better way," he wrote, "—if one has got to die . . . 30 seconds of horror and its [sic] all over,—for they say that it's all in that length of time, after a plane's been hit." Still, he felt fortunate to see the war from the air instead of from a muddy trench, and he took pride in the company of airmen. "There are some nice things about aviation, really," Quentin wrote. "It seems to be the one part of war in which brother Boche [a French insult for a German soldier] has the instincts of a sportsman and a gentleman."

Among themselves these gentleman pilots held to a code of honor. When an airman was shot down—on either side—he was given a military funeral. Such an honor, Quentin observed, was bestowed on the body of Germany's top pilot, the Red Baron, who had machine-gunned 80 Allied pilots from his Fokker aircraft.

Baron von Richthofen the German ace, was brought down by the English. They buried him with full military honors,—three French aces and three English aces for his pall bearers. It must have been most impressive, the French and English soldiers standing to attention as they lowered him into his grave.

Quentin took a break from flying to plan a Bastille Day celebration for people in a nearby town. He put together a "musical talent" to honor French Independence Day on July 14, rounding up a group of American servicemen who could play ragtime, complete with banjos. Quentin wouldn't have time to see the performance himself; he was scheduled to fly on the 14th. Full of good humor, he stopped by Ham Coolidge's billet, took a seat on the bed, and talked up the show to his friend. It promised to be a good time.

On Bastille Day, Quentin and other pilots sat in a briefing to learn their mission. Reports from the Château-Thierry sector said that the German army had begun its advance toward Paris. Quentin received instructions to tail and protect an observation plane as it flew over German territory taking photos of troops on the move. With the briefing over, Quentin walked out to the airfield and climbed into his Nieuport. A crewman yanked on its propeller to give it a start, and the airplane's single motor turned over and fired up. In moments the tiny airplane taxied down the grassy field and took off for the battle zone.

Early on Sunday morning, July 14, the *New York Times* reported that President Wilson had sent greetings to France in honor of Bastille Day. At home, Americans would celebrate with a big party of their own in Madison Square Garden. Another article said that the Red Cross Ambulance Corps had issued new gray uniforms to their drivers, women who delivered telegrams to families' doorsteps telling of dead or wounded soldiers.

From France came war news about General Pershing's growing forces: "More than eleven hundred thousand [American] soldiers are in the overseas army." Another story reported German and American activity in the Château-Thierry sector where Quentin was stationed, and evidence from the front showed that German machine gunners now used explosive bullets, "tearing a hole [in a man] instead of making the usual clean wound."

For the Roosevelts at Sagamore Hill, it was a summer Sunday with church and dinner, a day of rest and the beginning of a busy week. Theodore was scheduled to make a speech in Upstate New York a few days later. Edith and Ethel had children to look after and households to manage.

The next afternoon, Theodore Roosevelt was called to the door to meet an unexpected guest. There stood a family friend, Phil Thompson, a newspaperman in their local town of Oyster Bay. He looked uncertain, so Theodore motioned him to come inside so they could talk privately. Thompson held a cablegram that had been sent to the *New York Sun* and relayed on to him. Its contents had clearly been censored by the military. The cable said simply, "Watch Sagamore Hill for—" The rest had been deleted.

In a flash, Theodore knew that something had happened to one of his sons. Archie was in the hospital, and in all likelihood Ted was still recovering from the gas attack. That left Quentin. Without a word to Edith, Theodore saw his friend out the door. Gamely, he carried on as though no cablegram existed. He dressed for dinner and spent the evening with Edith, trying his best to let no flicker of concern cross his face. If Edith guessed that her husband was troubled, she did not tell him. But that night, Edith broke her nightly habit of writing in her diary, an unspoken clue that she suspected something was wrong.

The next morning, Phil Thompson returned. One look at his face, and Theodore had his answer. The Roosevelts' youngest child was dead. German fighters had shot down Quentin's plane behind enemy lines.

"But—Mrs. Roosevelt! How am I going to break it to her?" Theodore asked, posing the question more to himself than to

Phil Thompson. He turned away and walked inside, where he found Edith and told her the sad, awful truth. Phil waited on the stone patio. Indoors, Theodore sat down and wrote the most difficult words of his life. A half hour later, he came back outdoors with a statement for the press. Phil read the message that would go out on telegraph wires across the nation.

> Quentin's mother and I are very glad that he got to the front and had a chance to render some service to his country, and show the stuff that was in him before his fate befell him.

Heartbreaking days followed. Flora Whitney sat with the Roosevelts at Sagamore Hill to wait for more information, and Alice arrived from Washington. All the news from Europe traveled to New York over a cable that stretched across the bottom of the Atlantic Ocean. No one could be sure what had happened. Eleanor cabled Sagamore Hill that Quentin's death was "absolutely unconfirmed." Dick Derby relayed a rumor that Quentin might be alive and held prisoner. But in his heart of hearts, Theodore Roosevelt knew that Quentin had died.

Still waiting for confirmation from army officials, Theodore kept his promise to speak at the New York Republican state convention in Saratoga. Just two days after he had received the awful cable, Theodore took the podium in front of hundreds of people. He read from the speech he had written ahead of time until something took hold of his soul. The grieving father, who never mentioned his dead son to the crowd that day, spoke from his heart.

> The finest, the bravest, the best of our young men have sprung eagerly forward to face death for the sake of a high idea; and thereby they have brought home to us the great truth that life consists of more than easygoing pleasures,

The *Chicago Sunday Tribune* on August 4, 1914, shows photos of the five Roosevelts, along with a photo of Kaiser Wilhelm and his sons, to illustrate "The Difference Between Democracy and Autocracy."

541.9-011, Theodore Roosevelt Collection, Houghton Library, Harvard University and more than hard, conscienceless, brutal striving after purely material success.

On Saturday afternoon, nearly a week after Quentin was shot down, the family received "the final and definite announcement that he was killed and not captured." Theodore wrote to Kermit. "There is not much to say. . . . No man could have died in finer or more gallant fashion; and our pride equals our sorrow— . . . It is dreadful that the young should die."

It was some small comfort that Quentin had died instantly; a German pilot had shot him twice through the head. Theodore grieved for Quentin's fiancée, "poor, darling heartbroken Flora." It was tragic, the sad father thought, that Flora had been forbidden to go to France to marry Quentin. "Then they could have had their white hour," he wrote to a friend. Theodore ached for young Flora, who would never have a memory of making love with Quentin. Flora and Quentin had kept to the code of society to wait until after they were married.

Quentin Roosevelt Had Soldier Burial reported the *New York Times* on July 21. The Roosevelts read the official word that the Germans had buried Quentin with full military honors where his plane hit the ground. Like so many others in his family before him, Quentin would lie where he fell. The German honor guard knew that Quentin was the famous Theodore Roosevelt's son. Perhaps for that reason, a German photographer made a photograph of the dead pilot's body as it lay next to his wrecked airplane. Eventually a copy of the photo reached his parents.

Letters of sorrow made their way to Sagamore Hill. One came from Britain's King George V, while others came from everyday Americans. Roosevelt replied to one from a Mrs. Harvey Freeland that especially touched his heart:

It is hard to open the letters coming from those you love who are dead; but Quentin's last letters, written during

Quentin Roosevelt's body was laid out and photographed in front of his crashed plane.

Quentin Roosevelt plane crash. July 1918. Sagamore Hill National Historic Site. http://www.theodorerooseveltcenter.org/Research/Digital-Library/Record.aspx?libID =0276728. Theodore Roosevelt Digital Library. Dickinson State University.

his three weeks at the front, when of his squadron on an average a man was killed every day, are written with real joy in the "great adventure." He was engaged to a very beautiful girl, of very fine and high character; it is heartbreaking for her, as well as for his mother; but they both said that they would rather have him never come back than never have gone. He had his crowded hour, he died at the crest of life, in the glory of the dawn.

My other three boys are just as daring; and if the war lasts they will all be killed unless they are so crippled as to be sent home. Archie apparently has been crippled by his two shell wounds, but has been struggling against being sent home. Ted has been gassed, and is now with his gallant little wife in Paris, with two bullet wounds; he will be back at the front in a few weeks. Kermit won the British Military cross in Mesopotamia, but is now under Pershing. My son in law, Dick Derby, a major in the Medical Corps, has been knocked down by a shell, but after a week in hospital is back at the front. A good record, isn't it?

On Sunday morning July 21, Theodore and Edith went to their regular service at Christ Episcopal Church in their small town of Oyster Bay. From his pulpit, their rector spoke in memory of Quentin—a brave young man who had died for his nation. A few blocks away, the priest and worshippers at St. Dominic's Catholic Church asked prayers for the repose of Quentin's soul. In a local park in Oyster Bay, the American flag stood at half-mast. Under it flew a service flag dotted with 321 stars, one for each local citizen serving in the war. On the border was a lone gold star for Quentin, the first "boy from Oyster Bay to give his life for his country."

The Roosevelt family had made good its devotion to duty, honor, and sacrifice in the Great War. Theodore died in his sleep the following January—of a broken heart, some said. Edith lived another 40 years, until she died at 87, and she kept a piece of Quentin's crashed Nieuport with her at Sagamore Hill. Flora Whitney went on to marry one of Quentin's fellow pilots and had two children, but the marriage was unhappy and they divorced. Flora remarried and had two more children, and this time her marriage survived. With her mother, she used her wealth to found the Whitney Museum of Art in New York City.

Duty, honor, and sacrifice. Twenty-three years after Quentin died, his brothers fought Germany, Italy, and Japan in World War II. Archie saw action in the Pacific, where he was shot in the same knee that had taken a bullet during World War I. Kermit, struggling against deep depression and alcoholism, went to war in Alaska and killed himself with a pistol. Ted, keeping quiet about the pains in his chest, went back into the army as a brigadier general and commanded the landing at Utah Beach in the Normandy Invasion on D-day.

In classic Roosevelt form, Ted went ashore with the first wave of men early in the morning on D-day, June 6, 1944. Once on the beach, Ted could see they were more than a mile from their intended target. Leaning on a cane and facing heavy fire from German defenses, Ted limped back and forth across the sand, studied the situation, and was heard to say, "We'll start the war from right here!" His division—20,000 men and 1,700 vehicles—did exactly that and by nightfall stood firm on French soil.

A few days later, Ted Roosevelt felt crushing pain in his chest and dropped dead of a heart attack. He was buried at the foot of a white cross in the American Cemetery at Normandy, one among thousands of white crosses and Stars of David marking graves of Americans who fell on D-day. A gold star on General Theodore Roosevelt's cross distinguished it from the rest. After he died, the United States awarded Ted the Congressional Medal of Honor, the nation's ultimate honor for valor in wartime. Like father, like son—former president Theodore Roosevelt was granted the Medal of Honor after his death, as well.

In 1955, the remaining Roosevelts made a quiet request that was granted. From the field where his plane had crashed, Quentin's remains were moved to Normandy. There they were laid to rest in the grave just next to Ted's. Their mother would have wanted it that way.

Their father might have said, "A good record, isn't it?"

THE RED CAP

* * *

HENRY LINCOLN JOHNSON

> Henry Lincoln Johnson (1897–1929) worked as a red cap—a
> luggage porter—at a railway station in Albany, New York,
> when the United States entered World War I. He enlisted in the
> 15th Regiment of the New York National Guard, made up of
> African Americans. Forbidden to fight with white Americans
> in France, the men of the 15th were transferred to the French
> army's 369th Régiment, where they distinguished themselves
> in battle.

His French rifle held a full clip with three bullets. His long
bolo knife sat in its sheath. Grenades lay in a row at his feet,
deep in a trench that reached far above his head. Wide awake in
the moonlight at two o'clock in the morning on May 15, 1918,
Henry Lincoln Johnson, sergeant, US Army, was ready. Ready
for any sight or sound of an enemy German making his way
through the tangle of barbed wire and fence posts that spread
across the no-man's-land between the worn-out French army
and its German foes. Ready to shoot, throw grenades, fight with

his knife, use his bare hands if need be. In this godforsaken land of bullets and trenches and mud and needle-sharp wire, the rule was kill or be killed.

Henry shared sentry duty with Private Needham Roberts, another black soldier. Like Henry, Private Roberts watched and waited as the rest of their tiny outpost in the Argonne Forest, five men in all, slept in a bunker nearby. The last two nights had been quiet with no sign of a German intruder. But out here in the dead of night, when the fence posts and wire and mist rising from the mud could make a man think he was seeing a ghost or two, it was easy to miss something. At least Henry and the others from his regiment didn't worry about their faces shining in the moonlight like white soldiers, who had to smear grease all over their faces before they went on night duty.

Needham Roberts heard a sound, a click he thought, or was it just a rat scurrying along the duckboards that lined the trench? Roberts slinked from his end of the trench to Henry's, made the sign for silence, and led his trench mate back to listen for himself. Then more clicks, and they knew it was no rat—it was the sound of wire cutters, not in front but to their rear. A German raiding party had circled around and sneaked up behind them.

Just three weeks' training had prepared Henry and Needham for this moment, and they reacted exactly as they'd practiced: Henry fired a flare that lit up the night and both men screamed "Corporal of the Guard!"

No more secrecy for the Germans, who opened attack with a volley of grenades that found their marks. Needham went down, badly injured in both shoulder and hip, but he struggled to sit up so he could throw grenades at the oncoming Germans. Henry was hurt, too. Blood streamed from shrapnel cuts all over his body, but still he got to his feet with his rifle as a German soldier stormed into his trench. No stranger to a fight, the street-tough red cap from Albany opened fire. One shot. Two. Then three, which Henry fired point-blank at the intruder's chest. With a

Henry Johnson.
National Archives and Records
Administration, 533523

burst of blood from his gray uniform, the man fell and died.

Now a second German faced
Henry. Raiding parties didn't
wear helmets, so all the man
wore was a soft cap. With no
time to reload, Henry swung
his rifle around and hit him over
the head. Much to Henry's sur-
prise, the German swore at him in perfect English. "The little
black so-and-so has got me!"

"Yes, and this little black so-and-so'll get you again—if you
get up!" Henry warned, as he kept up his call. "Corporal of the
Guard!"

The Battle of Henry Johnson was on.

★ ★ ★

Just three years earlier, Henry couldn't have dreamed he'd be
fighting for the French army on a battlefield along the Marne
River. It was a long way from his job as a porter carrying passengers' bags at Union Central Station in Albany, New York. In
the United States in 1915, serving as a red cap was a good job
for a young black man who had come north from his home-
town of Alexandria, Virginia, to look for work. Henry Johnson
was but one soul in a great migration of African American
women and men who left their lives as second-class citizens in
the South and moved to big cities like Chicago, Kansas City,
New York, and Albany.

Life in the North was tough for black citizens like Henry Johnson. On paper, Henry and other people of color had the same rights as whites, but few of them could expect to find professional jobs in white-owned offices or work as teachers, doctors, or nurses in schools and hospitals quietly designated "whites only." Blacks could work at factory jobs or in hotels as doormen, elevator operators, waiters, or maids. The railroads did their part to hire black workers, mostly as red caps or cooks. A few lucky men made it all the way to the top as conductors.

In Albany, Henry made himself a new life. In 1915, as he hustled back and forth with leather suitcases and heavy trunks, he heard newsboys cry out headlines from the war in France. But Henry felt far removed from any battle. To most Americans, the Great War wasn't a problem. It was a fight between one side, made up of England and France and some Italians and Russians, and the other side—Germany and an empire by the name of Austria-Hungary. The battlefields of France, where Europe's young men had fought and died by the millions already, were an ocean away—very far from Albany. Besides, Henry and other Americans already had assurances from the top man in government that they were safe from the fighting. President Woodrow Wilson, now running for a second term, saw no need for the United States to take sides and had pledged neutrality to "keep America out of war."

But by the winter of 1917, all that would change. Now the headlines said that Germany would resume submarine attacks against American ships. In March, Americans learned that a secret telegram between German and Mexican diplomats spoke of Germany's plans to invade Texas. War fever spiked in Americans. Even the isolationist President Wilson, whose professorial personality made him more of a dreamer than a realist, was caught up in the outcry. On April 6, he asked the US Congress for a declaration of war. Most congressmen and senators were happy to oblige.

Young and old, black Americans like Henry Johnson showed up at recruiting stations to enlist and fight in France. Standing naked in front of a health inspector at five feet four inches in his bare feet, Henry barely made the cut. But at a fit 140 pounds and in every way a strong, healthy man, Henry was ordered to report for training with the 15th (Colored) Regiment of the New York National Guard. Johnson didn't know that he would be part of an experiment conducted by the US Army. The 15th would be a black-only regiment. If Johnson and his fellow soldiers proved themselves, they just might get the opportunity to fight in France.

Colored and *Negro* were considered polite terms to describe black soldiers in the United States at the time. African Americans had a long and distinguished history of fighting for their country from its beginning in the American Revolution. Yet in 1917, debates in the halls of government, in the White House, and among the top brass in the War Department questioned whether black men were fit to fight in combat. Certainly they were strong enough to build camps, dig trenches, load and unload ships on the docks, cook, clean, and work as servants. But fight—were they capable of that? And would white soldiers be willing to fight alongside them?

Such were the questions asked in Washington. Yet some military men who believed that blacks had every right to fight in the war asked for an opportunity to prove they were right. They included an outspoken officer, Colonel William Hayward, an upper-crust lawyer who got a go-ahead from the governor to lead a brand-new "colored" regiment. New York's armories (large, airy buildings where national guardsmen trained and stored their weapons) were already spoken for, so Hayward and his senior officers, all white as agreed upon, set up shop in an empty dance hall in Brooklyn.

Eventually 1,200 African American soldiers, Henry Johnson and Needham Roberts among them, enlisted in the 15th New

York Regiment, and their officers began to equip them with uniforms and weapons. Rifles arrived, but only a fourth of them were topped with bayonets. It was no secret that the United States was unprepared for war, whether it was troopships or cannons or Springfield rifles made in nearby Massachusetts. President Wilson and his Democratic administration had long been called out by war hawks like former president Theodore Roosevelt. The old Rough Rider had worried about Germany's massive war machine for years and predicted that the United States would be dragged into battle.

In 1915 and 1916, Roosevelt's four sons had answered their father's call to prepare for war by going to summer camps in Plattsburgh, New York. One of those Plattsburgh volunteers, a Harvard graduate named Hamilton Fish Jr., jumped at Colonel Hayward's invitation to command the black soldiers and joined the 15th as a captain. Fish, a well-off New Yorker with a famous name, was broader-minded than most about the potential of black soldiers to perform well in battle.

A Harvard man like all of the Roosevelts, Hamilton Fish captained Harvard's football team and was a two-time All American. The Fish family had served in government since the revolution. Hamilton Fish's cousin, who shared the same name, was remembered as the first among Theodore Roosevelt's Rough Riders to die at the Battle of San Juan Hill during the Spanish-American War. His mother traced her ancestry back to Peter Stuyvesant, the first Dutch governor of colonial New York.

By contrast, Henry Johnson's ancestors had arrived on slave ships from Africa. The other black soldiers in his regiment came from many walks of life—a preacher, a burglar, other railroad porters and bellhops like Henry and Needham, and even a big-time jazz player named Jim Europe. But not one of these men really knew his roots.

Men like Johnson and Roberts and Hayward and Fish built the 15th New York from the bottom up, drilling in the old hall that carried memories of laughing couples dancing and drinking beer. "It started without traditions, without education, and without friends," wrote an officer in later years. The colonel counted on his officers to understand military procedure and protocol as they carried out every bit of training by themselves. Until after the war, not one instructor came from outside their own group to teach them anything. If any regiment had to raise itself by its bootstraps, it was the 15th New York, nicknamed early on as the Heavy Foot. No campaign ribbons hung from the unit's flags to proudly display an honored past. Such awards might come in time—once they'd proved their battle worthiness in France.

Henry Johnson, his fellow infantrymen, and their commanding officers faced obstacles from the start. Colonel Hayward begged his superiors to make his regiment part of the Rainbow Division, a giant collection of regiments headed to camp for specialized war training. But the answer was no. Black was not a color of the rainbow, his superiors said, and no black soldiers were going to France to fight side by side with white soldiers. When the New York National Guard held a farewell parade, the 15th was denied permission to march in it. Colonel Hayward snarled, damned the whole going-away party, and promised that on the day his regiment returned from France, his men would march in a parade that would go down in history.

The colonel launched a one-man campaign to secure war training for his men. Letters flew, filled with complaints about unfair and downright stupid treatment of his soldiers. He pointed out that his capable fighting men, who had finished their basic training, were now scattered about New York guarding railway bridges, ammunition compounds, and navy ships. It was clear that his soldiers had been pushed to the back of the pipeline that fed the army's training camps for battle overseas— only because they were Negroes.

Someone at the top finally listened to Colonel Hayward's plea, and he received his longed-for orders. Two battalions of the 15th were to board a troop train for camp in Spartanburg, South Carolina, to learn the skills of warfare. But there was a problem. Spartanburg sat in the Deep South, where Jim Crow laws segregated blacks from whites. Trouble was sure to find the black soldiers from the North. One step across the color line that ran through Spartanburg society and a black soldier could find himself in the hands of a white mob ready with a rope to lynch him.

Such were the dangers and the insults black fighting men like Henry Johnson and Needham Roberts had faced even before they sailed for France. But the insults faded a bit once they came ashore from the *Pocahontas*, their troopship. Here in France there was no color line. There were lots of other men of color in the French forces, mostly colonial recruits from North Africa. Rumors flew that the Germans feared these dark-skinned fighters, who were said to kill every man they captured.

Henry Johnson and his fellow black soldiers didn't need to worry whether the French army would judge them by their dark skin. When Henry stopped at a café or walked along a French street, he didn't have to step out of the way to allow a white man to pass him. Why, here in France, it was perfectly fine for a black soldier to have a white girl on his arm!

However, as open as French society and the French army seemed to be, the US Army still segregated its black soldiers. Colonel Hayward had managed to elevate his men to fighting status, but once they landed in France to join General John Pershing's American Expeditionary Forces, his hopes blew up. General Pershing followed the orders issued by his commander in chief, President Wilson, who refused to mix white soldiers with blacks. The men from New York again were put to work as common laborers and dockworkers.

Pershing had other concerns. The French army, bleeding out from battlefield casualties and huge numbers of deserters, insisted that the fresh-faced, well-fed Americans pouring into the AEF must come under French command. The proud General Pershing would have none of that—until the 15th arrived with its black soldiers, offering him a way to solve his problem. He could please both President Wilson and the French by transferring this American regiment of black soldiers to the French army.

General Pershing saw his chance and took it. He ordered the transfer, and quite by surprise Henry and the others discovered one day that their 15th New York Infantry had a new name: the 369th *Régiment d'Infanterie, Américaine*. From Colonel Hayward at the top to men like Private Henry Johnson, the 369th came under the command of the 4th French army headed by General Henri Gouraud, who warmly greeted the black troops with the one arm he had. The French called the black soldiers *Les enfants perdu*, "the lost orphans."

***

But all that had passed weeks and months before, and in these predawn hours on May 15, 1918, Henry Johnson found himself in the fight of his life on a battlefield in France. As the English-speaking attacker lay stunned in the trench, Henry saw two other Germans who clearly were preparing to take his fellow soldier prisoner. Henry leaped to the side, yanking his bolo knife from its sheath. Knees bent, he landed on the shoulders of the crouching German and thrust the machete-like blade through the man's skull. When it could sink no farther, Henry yanked it out. By now the knocked-down soldier was back on his feet, his Luger automatic pistol spitting bullets. Henry took a hit, a "burning, stinging pain" that brought him down on hands and knees—for a moment. Catching the gunman off guard, Henry rose up, swung his blade into the German's belly, and gutted him.

The Germans panicked and began to retreat. They loaded their injured onto stretchers and started back toward their own line. Henry, bleeding and angry as a wounded grizzly, climbed up to where he could pelt the retreating enemy with grenades. Then he passed out.

A relief party finally arrived. Henry faded in and out of consciousness, mumbling "Corporal of the Guard" as he and Needham Roberts were loaded onto a mule-drawn railroad flatcar. One of his officers, Captain Arthur Little, threw on rubber boots and a raincoat over his pajamas and raced to meet them at the dressing station. There, both the wounded men were talking as they sipped sweet, mind-numbing cups of rum kept for times like this. "I feared that these men would die," the captain wrote. "They were wounded in so many places." But Henry Johnson waved his hand at the captain, because he had something to say. "Sir Captain Sir," he said in his low husky voice with the familiar accent of a Southern black man, "you all don't want to worry 'bout me. I'm all right. I've been shot before!"

When day dawned, officers headed to the scene of Henry Johnson's attack to figure out exactly what had happened. They tracked the Germans' path backward for half a mile. It was littered with blood-soaked bandages, pistols, wire cutters, and 40 unexploded grenades. Marks on the ground showed that two stretchers had been carried back. Typically the Germans assigned a stretcher to every dozen men. At least 24 Germans had made up the raiding party that descended on Henry Johnson.

Just a week after the raid, the US Army's own newspaper, the *Stars and Stripes*, broke the story to other soldiers in General Pershing's American Expeditionary Forces. Two Black Yanks Smear 24 Huns; Big Secret Out, ran the headline. Station Porter and Elevator Boy Win Croix de Guerre.

In the meantime, Irvin Cobb, a crusty magazine writer from Kentucky, decided to see for himself if the stories he heard were true. Were black American troops actually in the trenches

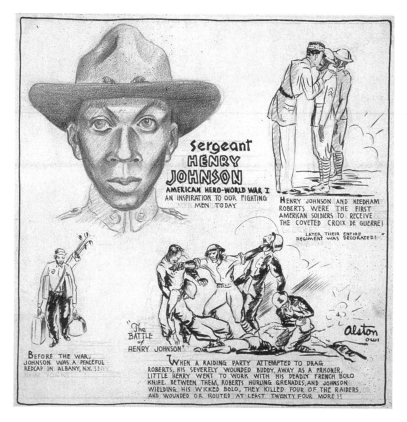

Years later, during World War II, the US government would tell the story of Henry Lincoln Johnson to promote the war effort.

National Archives and Records Administration, NARA 535680

fighting for France? The Southern journalist viewed the aftermath of Johnson's battle, including a pool of blood the size of a five-gallon punch bowl that would not drain in the chalky clay soil. His article about Henry Johnson appeared in the *Saturday Evening Post* later that summer.

Henry Johnson and Needham Roberts received the French medal of valor. With a kiss to each cheek, a French officer pinned them with the Croix de Guerre trailing a red-and-green-striped ribbon. Across Henry's medal lay a gold palm, a special sign of honor.

Both soldiers survived their ordeal. Henry had multiple wounds and spent weeks in the hospital. Surgeons removed many small bones from his shattered foot and inserted a metal plate in their place; from then on, Henry's foot slapped the floor as he limped. His fighting days were over, and he could have been medically discharged and sent home to Albany, but he asked to stay. His commanding officers kept him on as a sort of mascot to cheer their men. Roberts returned to battle and survived the war.

By the end of the war on November 11, 1918, the battle-hardened black soldiers of the 369th *Régiment* had fought their way across France to the banks of the Rhine in Germany.

They were the first Americans to reach Germany's legendary river. Though hundreds of men lost their lives, the regiment never gave up one bit of ground to the German army. Not one man was taken prisoner, nor did the regiment allow any of its prisoners to escape. The Heavy Foot regiment from New York earned a new nickname as well. On Armistice Day, Henry Johnson stood at roll call as a proud member of the Harlem Hellfighters.

Needham Roberts wears the Croix de Guerre, France's highest combat medal.
Library of Congress, LC-USZ62-104346

Colonel Hayward made good on his promise. When the regiment arrived home in New York, the black veterans were the first wave of returning soldiers to parade all the way through Manhattan and on up north to Harlem. Marching French army–style in phalanxes, tight columns of helmeted soldiers gave New Yorkers their first view of the black soldiers who had been denied a farewell parade less than two years earlier. Once they got to Harlem, the colonel permitted his men to march in an open platoon formation so that onlookers could spot their husbands, sons, brothers, and boyfriends. Singing and laughing, many of the soldiers took their sweethearts by the hand as the Hellfighters marched through Harlem.

Henry Johnson rode in an open car that filled up with flowers as the marchers wound through Manhattan. Then Henry disappeared, AWOL—absent without leave. When he showed up three days later, he had to stand in front of his officers to explain why. He told them a story that made them smile. After the parade, Henry explained, "he had been taken in charge by a group of gentlemen, who had taken him successively to a number of Fifth Avenue clubs and hotels, where he had been entertained with food and drink and rewarded with money." How could he refuse their generosity, especially since many of them were friends of these very officers? As proof of his story, Henry pulled out a wad of cash—$600 or more.

Henry was forgiven for his three-day binge, dismissed with honor from the army, and sent home. For a time, he was the man of the hour in Albany. He spoke of returning to his old job as a red cap. But time wasn't good to this *enfant perdu*. Though he had made it home to Albany, Henry Lincoln Johnson became a casualty of World War I. A hero to the French and to his own race at home, Henry didn't amount to much in the eyes of most white Americans. As his fame faded, he took to drinking and became addicted to alcohol. First he lost his ability to work, and then he became estranged from his family.

Over time, Henry's family lost track of him. He drifted from place to place until 1929, when he died in an Illinois veteran's hospital at the age of 32. Someone saw fit to ship his body to Arlington National Cemetery in Virginia, where Henry Lincoln Johnson was laid to rest—but under a different name. Far off in Paris, the American art critic Gertrude Stein was a keen observer of the young men and women whom war had changed. A tough older woman who had driven ambulances in France, she had picked up on a phrase that described these wayward young folks perfectly. "You are all a lost generation," she told the writer Ernest Hemingway, who at 18 had nearly died on the Italian front. Henry Johnson fit that mold, and he became a member of the Lost Generation of World War I survivors.

Folks said that Needham Roberts never got over his war experiences either and that he spent the end of his days in an asylum for the mentally ill.

Henry's son Herman followed his father's example and served in the US military as a member of the Tuskegee Airmen, black pilots who joined the Army Air Corps to fight Germany and Japan in World War II. Like Henry, Lieutenant Johnson was forbidden to fly with white pilots in combat. Instead, the Tuskegee Airmen flew cargo and ferried airplanes at home in the United States. Not until 1948 did another World War I veteran, President Harry S. Truman, sign an executive order that banished segregation in the United States Armed Forces.

Herman Johnson also sought recognition for his father's war accomplishments.

Wounded World War I veterans could apply for Purple Hearts when the US military began awarding them in 1932. Henry Johnson had been entitled to the award after his death, but it was not until 1996 that he—and Needham Roberts— finally received their Purple Hearts posthumously.

Yet Henry's family still didn't know what had happened to him. Herman Johnson spent years searching for his father's unmarked grave, which his family assumed was somewhere near the Albany airport.

Then, in 2002, the Johnson family learned that Henry's grave had been located at Arlington National Cemetery. An old record showed the gravesite had been assigned to a William Henry Johnson. At a later time, someone had crossed out "William." The rest of the information about the buried soldier at Arlington matched Henry Lincoln Johnson's perfectly, and Henry was no longer lost to his family. Or so it seemed at the time.

Herman Johnson never gave up trying to win his father the recognition that he deserved for his heroic act in France. In 2002, the army agreed to award Henry Lincoln Johnson the Distinguished Service Cross. Still, the Johnson family pushed on with their campaign to secure Henry the Congressional Medal of Honor, the nation's highest award for heroism in military service. A high-level general rejected their bid, because there was no US Army document to support their case. Technically, Henry Johnson had fought for the French.

Then in 2011, a staffer working for a New York senator launched a web search that turned up a crucial piece of evidence to bolster the Johnsons' case. As she scrolled through an online database, the staffer discovered a memo from General Pershing dated May 20, 1918. Pershing had cited Henry Johnson's "notable instance of bravery and devotion" six days earlier. It was a remarkable discovery, the missing link that the Johnson family needed to achieve their goal.

On June 2, 2015, Henry Johnson was awarded the Congressional Medal of Honor by President Barack Obama. The president recognized Henry and one other serviceman for their heroism in rescuing comrades on the battlefields of France nearly a century ago.

But that day was bittersweet for the Johnson family. An army investigation into Henry's background had led to a disappointing discovery. Henry was apparently childless and not Herman

Johnson's biological father, although Herman had lived his life believing so. Henry's real name, the research showed, was William Henry Johnson, as it had been documented at Arlington. Moreover, another family had stepped forward to claim Johnson as their own. In the century since Henry's act of valor, much of his story had become lost or confused.

Though the news was "devastating," Herman's daughter Tara attended the medal ceremony. But she wasn't a blood relative, so it was left to a present-day member of Henry's old unit, the 369th Infantry Regiment, to receive the medal on his behalf.

Perhaps further research will uncover more of the truth about the man known as Henry Lincoln Johnson.

THE PITCHER

★ ★ ★

CHRISTY MATHEWSON

> *In 1918 Christopher "Christy" Mathewson (1880–1925) was one of the nation's most respected baseball players, both on and off the field.*

He was a college player in a day when just a handful of kids graduated from high school.

He became the star pitcher for the New York Giants who, along with manager John J. McGraw, brought his team to greatness.

He pitched three shutouts in a five-game World Series.

He was the "Big 6."

He was "Matty."

He was the "Idol of All Fandom."

He took his own turn as manager for the Cincinnati Reds.

At the grand old age of 36, he'd done it all.

But he hadn't served his country. When the call came in 1918, Christy Mathewson said yes and joined the American Expeditionary Forces in France.

As a kid growing up in Factoryville, Pennsylvania, in the 1880s and '90s, Christopher "Christy" Mathewson learned the game of baseball, a sport already entrenched in the American imagination. He was said to practice his flaming pitch by hurling baseballs through a small hole in a barn wall, and he began playing semipro ball at age 14 in 1895.

Christy Mathewson didn't smoke, but that didn't stop a tobacco company from idolizing him and Ty Cobb in its advertising. *Author's Collection*

Christy pitched for Bucknell University for the two years he went to college. At Bucknell he was sweet on a girl, but she thought her friend Jane Stoughton would make a better match, so she set them up. Christy and Jane dated and got married in 1903. For the rest of their days, Jane followed him devotedly as he moved from town to town making his way up the ranks of Major League Baseball.

In 1900, at age 19, he joined the majors to pitch for the New York Giants. At six foot one and 195 pounds, Christy looked every bit the "Big 6"—his number—as his baseball career moved ever higher. He stood as the game's leading pitcher. He was the first pitcher in the 20th century to win 30 games in three successive years, including 1908, when he won 37. Damon Runyon, a young reporter who was the same age as Christy, said of the star, "Mathewson pitched against Cincinnati yesterday. Another way of putting it is that Cincinnati lost a game of baseball. The first statement means the same as the second."

Honored among fans and sportswriters as the "Christian gentleman," Christy upheld a long-ago promise he'd made to his mother, a strict Baptist who ruled that Sundays were for going to church and not for playing sports. He didn't object to Sunday ballgames, but he honored his mother by never pitching on the Sabbath.

Others in the game admired the star pitcher for his honesty. Cheating in baseball was part of the sport when he took the mound for the Giants in 1900. All around him, pitchers and hitters were said to "throw" games in return for cash payouts. Over the 16 years that Matty pitched for the Giants, his reputation stayed clean as a whistle.

By 1916 his best pitching days were over, and Matty took a new job managing the Cincinnati Reds. He was bringing his new team up to speed when the United States declared war on Germany in April 1917. In a flash, America's favorite pastime took second place to war fever, as young men from cities, suburbs, farms, and ranches stood in line to sign up with the AEF and head to France, where they'd get into the war against Germany and "Kaiser Bill."

The Germans had launched a new and deadly evil against Allied Forces in April 1915 during the Second Battle of Ypres: artillery shells filled not with explosives and shrapnel but with chlorine gas, a poisonous yellow-green cloud flowing along the ground. Five thousand French soldiers had choked and died from the chemical. Countless others suffered scorched lungs and burned eyes. On both sides of the war, the use of poison gas mushroomed, as armies filled their stockpiles with deadly chemicals designed to destroy airways and lungs (chlorine and phosgene), blister the skin (mustard gas), or poison the bloodstream (hydrogen cyanide).

Early in 1918 the United States government consolidated the nation's chemical warfare research into a branch of the War Department. The brand-new Chemical Warfare Service (CWS) rapidly added 1,600 army officers and 18,000 enlisted men to its ranks. Its top commander, General William Sibert, recruited proven leaders, men strong in both mind and body who were "endowed with extraordinary capabilities to lead others during gas attacks."

Baseball's top players and officials dropped their bats and gloves and scorecards and went to France. Matty wound up in the same unit as another baseball legend, Ty Cobb. Both wore captain's bars on their shoulders. A former player-turned-manager, Branch Rickey wore the insignia of major, outranking them both. All three served as instructors in the CWS "Gas and Flame Division" at Hanlon Field near Chaumont, France. Second Lieutenant Joseph T. Hanlon had been the first CWS American to die in action, and the army had honored him by giving his name to its chemical weapons testing center.

Matty and Ty Cobb trained hundreds of soldiers. "We wound up drilling the damnedest bunch of culls [rejects] that

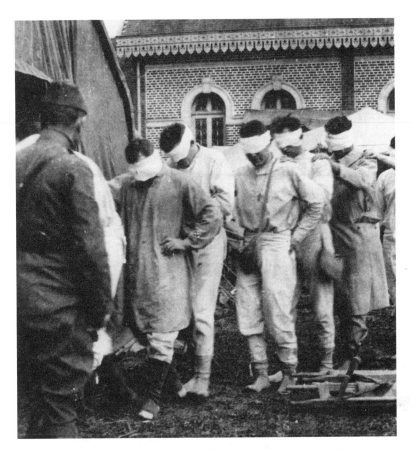

Blinded by a gas attack, American soldiers are led into a medical treatment station. *McCormick Research Center*

World War I ever grouped in one outfit," said Ty Cobb later. Apparently the US Army believed that Cobb, Matty, and other professional athletes stood a better chance than most officers of earning their men's respect. Cobb reported that "those that gave us trouble and didn't heed orders didn't last long, for we weren't fooling around with simulated death when we entered the gas chambers. The stuff we turned loose was the McCoy [the real thing]."

But it wasn't all work in France. Officers and enlisted alike brought baseball with them and tried introducing their beloved game to the French, who weren't interested. Folks at home learned why when Matty spoke to newspapermen once he returned.

Baseball will never be a popular game in France, I'm afraid. The French think it is brutal. There were plenty of games between American doughboys and French poilus [infantrymen], but the schedule never lasted long, because you couldn't get a Frenchman to act as catcher.

Out in the street one day some of our men were playing a game. The pitcher, on one sidewalk, was shooting them over pretty hard at the catchers, on the other sidewalk. Traffic was blocked in a few minutes. None of the French would walk behind the catcher. They were deathly afraid he would miss the ball. It looked faster than a bullet to them.

The next day's edition of the paper added more.

Their infield work is rotten. Every time a Frenchman gets behind a bat he wants to retreat about 10 paces, erect a barbed wire entanglement, dig himself a dug out and crawl into it.

No, the Frenchman will never take to baseball in a big way. He prefers something gentle, such as football [soccer] and dueling.

Playing ball offered a much-needed break for the men of the Chemical Warfare Service. Their mission was deadly serious. The Allies' original gas masks, Ty noted, were "a joke at first . . . cumbersome affairs" with mask, nose clips, mouth tube, and canisters hanging from the soldier's neck. By 1918, however, technology had improved, gas masks with them, so now the CWS trained men inside gas chambers—sealed, airtight rooms. "At a hand signal," Ty explained, "everyone was supposed to snap his mask into position. Alertness and speed was the goal."

I'll never be able to forget the day when some of the men—myself included—missed the signal.

Men screamed to be let out when they got a sudden whiff of the sweet death in the air. They went crazy with fear and in the fight to get out jammed up in a hopeless tangle.

As soon as I realized what had happened, but only after inhaling some gas, I fixed my mask, groped my way to the wall and worked through the thrashing bodies to the door. Trying to lead the men out was hopeless. It was each one of us in there for himself.

Cobb had no clue whether his lungs were damaged. For weeks he coughed up a colorless discharge until, finally, his lungs cleared. "Divine Providence" had touched him, he believed, but it did not touch all the others, "[f]or sixteen men were stretched on the ground after the training exercise and eight of them died."

Matty survived the accident but said, "Ty, when we were in there, I got a good dose of that stuff. I feel terrible." Matty wheezed as he breathed and blew out congested matter from his lungs.

"I saw Christy Mathewson doomed to die," wrote Ty Cobb. "None of us who were with him at the time realized that the rider on the pale horse had passed his way. Nor did Matty, the greatest National League pitcher of them all."

With the war's end, Matty came home to Jane and their son, Christy Jr., and resumed his old life in baseball. He went back to the New York Giants as "right hand man" to John McGraw and

Baseball greats Christy Mathewson (left) and Ty Cobb served
together in the "Gas and Flame"
Division of the Chemical Warfare Service.
National Baseball Hall of Fame Library,
Cooperstown, New York

then became president of
the Boston Braves in 1923.

But the coughing never
stopped, and soon enough,
it was evident that he had
contracted tuberculosis. He
spent months at a time at a
sanatorium in Upstate New
York to "take the cure,"
sleeping out of doors in the
bitter cold, eating well, and
staying in bed—all per his doctor's orders. It was a frustrating
experience for an active man like Matty, but as with all the challenges in life, he met this one head-on. Wrote Ty Cobb:

> He had a will, did Mathewson. "When a fellow can't read
> or write or talk and [can] barely move," he'd say, "it takes
> a little doing to keep his mind off his troubles. So I've
> started working out a baseball game, on paper. I figure
> the odds on any given play, just the way it happens on the
> field. I spend every day at it and I've learned a lot about
> the game I didn't suspect."

There you had an old-time ball player talking. With
his body gone, his head never stopped working.

At the sanatorium, Matty became just as skilled in the game of checkers. He read books about checkers and studied all of its strategies and plays. He also took up another hobby: when his health improved and he was allowed to leave the sanatorium, Matty would drive into the country and walk through the woods and fields searching for wildflowers. Then he drew and cataloged them in a notebook.

In the spring of 1923, Matty was well enough to take on a new job as president of the Boston Braves, a team that had floundered for years. He pushed forward, working hard for the Braves and doing his best to beat the tuberculosis that would never go away. He seemed to be doing so much better, but he wasn't cured, as he warned a magazine writer in 1924. Tuberculosis was like that.

Then he caught a cold that turned into deadly pneumonia, and Matty's courageous life drew to an end on October 7, 1925. Always the gentleman, he was said to console Jane by telling her, "Now Jane, I want you to go outside and have yourself a good cry. Don't make it a long one—this can't be helped."

It was World Series time. The day after Matty died, the Pittsburgh Pirates and Washington Senators wore black armbands on their uniforms in his honor.

A decade later, in 1936, Christy Mathewson and Ty Cobb became two of the first five players inducted into the Baseball Hall of Fame. Ty Cobb's batting record still stands among the best in Major League Baseball, and Christy Mathewson is still one of the winningest pitchers of all time.

THE SHOWGIRL

* * *

ELSIE JANIS

Elsie Janis (1889–1956) was a household name when she became "the sweetheart of the AEF." She had been a child star who'd visited American presidents, performed on both sides of the Atlantic, and was a regular on the London stage. In 1917 she got her chance to do her part in the Great War.

To the A.E.F., with all my love,
      I dedicate this book,
And hope if they ever read it,
      They will smile with me and look
Back on the "good times" over there,
      And think only of the day
When after their work was done I came
      And then we would start to play.
Oh; it was fun, wasn't it, "fellahs"?
      I'll say it was "some swell guerre,"

For I lost my heart to each one of you
In the big show "Over There."

—Elsie Janis.

Four thousand doughboys stood by in a big locomotive roundhouse, a repair shed for American trains at Nevers, France. They crammed into the big building until it was so full the rest lined up along the tracks outside. A shout went up as they spotted a Baldwin steam locomotive rolling toward them. Cheers followed. Riding the cowcatcher on the front of the Baldwin stood a young woman dressed in a fluted skirt and black tam, waving as the locomotive puffed into the roundhouse. She jumped to the platform, did a handspring, and shouted, "Boys, are we downhearted?" They roared back their answer.

"Hell no!"

Elsie Janis, one of America's biggest stars, had just opened her show. She was an old hand at show business. Elsie got her start at age two and a half when she toddled onstage at church socials. Her mother, who went on to become a notorious "stage mother," promoted Elsie however she could. The little girl had a huge gift for imitating others and at an early age was making people laugh in the vaudeville halls of New York City. She could sing, dance, and act as well, so she moved on to the theater. Her enormous talent carried her far and wide—from the white lights of Broadway to packed houses in Europe.

Elsie was a regular in London and Paris when World War I broke out in the summer of 1914. Along with the audiences she entertained, Elsie witnessed the war firsthand, as most Americans could not. Elsie had unswerving loyalty to the Allies and a bitter disgust for "the Huns."

She took the threat of German submarines in stride, braving sea voyages back and forth across the Atlantic in order to fulfill her showbiz contracts. Elsie was stateside when she ginned up the idea of performing for the troops in France, and she talked up her plans to everyone she knew. "I started in at home, recruiting, playing benefits, and doing a very 'war-mad' act in vaudeville, singing patriotic songs, etcetera, and telling everyone I was going to France. No one quite believed it, and to me it seemed almost too good to be true, but it was!"

Elsie was one among the actresses, nurses, ambulance drivers, canteen workers, and telephone operators who took active roles in World War I. She was probably the most famous American woman to do her bit for her beloved "boys"—American doughboys, French poilus, and British Tommies.

In the fall of 1917, the 28-year-old Elsie was in London with her mother, their maid, and her pet Pekinese named Mousme. Elsie had only hazy explanations of her plans for France and felt she was "probably a little bit in the dark" about what would happen when she got across the channel and looked for ways to perform. But opportunity knocked, and she got into France without any kind of contract with the Red Cross or the YMCA. (Both relief organizations were officially sanctioned by the US Army. Eventually, there would be one million young Americans in France, and the army counted on the Y canteens, "huts" as they were called, to keep its soldiers busy and out of trouble when they weren't fighting.)

The YMCA had wind of her plans—Elsie Janis was too big a star to ignore, even if the US government hadn't given her its official approval. She arrived in Bordeaux and "was greeted by a pair of young men from the Young Men's Christian Association who were driving 'young Henry Fords' [American-built cars]." Elsie studied the Y's map of France, dotted with places where she could play to the troops.

Elsie had her doubts about the do-gooder reputation of the YMCA men and inquired sassily if her fans could come to her shows whether they were young Christians or not. She feared the organization would cramp her style, but she joined with the Y when officials assured her they had only "the boys" in mind. They called in a pianist, and Elsie started rehearsals that afternoon.

Three years into the war, suffering and privation met her wherever she went in France. "We had breakfast with—No meat, no bread except of dusky hue, no butter, no sugar no jam no nothing—and very little of that . . ." She slept at the classy Crillon Hotel in Paris, but things had changed since her earlier visits. Its clerks, elevator boys, and waiters wore medals, some with their eyes, arms, or even their legs missing. Still, they offered Elsie their smiles of welcome.

Elsie wrote about her wartime life in a brash, breezy style, much the same as her stage persona. But during all those months in France, she masked a secret. Elsie nursed a broken heart. In London she'd fallen in love with Basil Hallam Radford, a popular actor and singer who had shared the stage with the actress Billie Burke in New York. (Years later, Burke would play her stellar role as Glinda, the Good Witch of the North, in *The Wizard of Oz*.)

Radford had tried to enlist in the British Army several times, always rejected as "unfit," until finally the Flying Corps commissioned him as an officer. He died during the Battle of the Somme when his observation balloon drifted over enemy lines and came under fire. One observer parachuted to safety, but Basil Radford fell to his death.

Elsie regained some measure of happiness when the United States joined the fight against Germany. Unlike most women who worked at the front, she wangled her way out of wearing a uniform in France. In Provins, on their way to entertain 2,000 Americans at Chaumont, Elsie and her mother waited as their papers were examined by French officials, who nearly arrested them for spying. After all, Elsie was decked out in civilian clothes.

We went to the "gare," [train station] where a crowd of villagers gathered around us. . . . I began to feel like the spy who was condemned to be shot at sunrise and said, "But I never get up till ten." After waiting about half an hour, while the French driver went in to explain things, in his own sweet way, by saying that he knew nothing about us, he had been ordered to drive us to Chaumont and he was doing it, he finally came back with what we gleaned was the Boss of Provins.

Elsie and her mother were ordered back to Paris.

The train would leave in two hours and . . . we were very lucky to be allowed to go, as [we] really should go to the local Sing Sing [jail]. . . . [I]n the meantime the French would certainly have to answer to the US Army, two thousand of which were waiting in Chaumont to be sung to by the "super spy," Mlle. Elsie Janis! . . . When it came near train time the police came for us and we were escorted to the comic train by them, put into a carriage. . . . I made a speech from the carriage door to the Boss of Provins and all his staff, telling them that I did not blame them but that inside of two weeks we would come back to Provins with a blue passe. . . . We pulled out and left them standing with what a pity—so young and yet so false expression lurking under their beards and to add insult to injury they all yelled *Bonne chance!* [Good luck!]

Elsie made good on her promise. None other than General John Pershing ordered a car for her, and from then on she and her mother traveled France in a big Cadillac driven by an American soldier. Two weeks later, she was back in Provins with car and driver, duly impressing everyone who had treated her so rudely. Elsie shared the opinion of other Americans who'd had

Elsie Janis.

bad experiences and disliked the French, as she explained, "not because we did not like them but because we did not like their not liking us."

Elsie was a trooper and performed up to nine shows in one day. She entertained on makeshift stages and tabletops, and she felt just as comfortable taking her show into hospital wards. She always opened her act with that same question, "Are we downhearted?" Bold, brash, and talented, she sang, danced, did a few imitations, and cracked jokes for the troops.

Elsie's mother, Janice Bierbower, went everywhere with her daughter, to the annoyance of the French, who felt that even one woman at the front was one woman too many. The two were sleeping in a pair of makeshift rooms in the wee hours when noise outside awoke them both. Elsie had done two shows that evening and reached her room just in time to get out of pouring rain. Mixed in with the sound of rain, she heard the tramp-tramp-tramp of men on the march. It struck her that the army usually sent its troops to the front line during the night, and she threw open her shutters. Below her window she saw some of the young men she'd played to just a few hours before, ready to do their part in the "Big Show."

> I leaned out quietly and they kept coming—each little bunch humming their own tune or whistling—and when I heard three of my own songs I could no longer resist. I yelled out Atta boy! They did not dare stop, but some of them knew that funny voice of mine and they said, "So long, Elsie. Come back soon."

I was so carried away at being in on that just before dawn stuff and seeing those tin lids, gas masks, rifles, etc., all going one way that I did not realize my teeth were chattering or that Mother was standing beside me weeping quite silently. Between sniffs she said, "You should not stand there in your nightgown." And between sniffs I answered, "They couldn't see me." "Oh," she said, "I mean you will catch more cold," and then we both leaned out again, knowing that we shared the same thought that a cold didn't much matter when you thought of what those dear boys were going into—splashing through inches of mud—loaded down like pack-horses.

Elsie Janis was living in a Paris hotel when Germany launched long-range attacks with giant cannons nicknamed "Big Berthas." With a range of six miles, these German howitzers fired 1,800-pound shells that burrowed 40 feet into the ground before exploding. This photo shows victorious Americans posing with a captured Big Bertha.

National World War I Museum at Liberty Memorial

Elsie Janis and "her boys," dressed as World War I veterans from the United States, Britain, and France, reprise their war experiences in a show in 1920. *Author's collection*

Elsie kept performing on her own nickel until she needed to accept a paying gig on the London stage. She did her best to stay in touch with her beloved boys via telegram, including one she sent to the AEF during the Battles of Meuse-Argonne. "Congratulations on your big show. Sorry not to be in the cast. Hope to join the company in Berlin."

Elsie Janis continued to star on stage and also shared her talent on the silver screen. She applied her considerable gifts to writing hit songs, live shows, and screenplays. After her mother died, she married a man named Gilbert Wilson, and they moved to Hollywood in 1936. Elsie Janis won her star on the Hollywood Walk of Fame. She died in 1956.

THE KID

* * *

ERNEST HEMINGWAY

> *Ernest Hemingway (1899–1961), one of America's best-known authors, was just out of high school when he managed to get in on the Great War driving a Red Cross ambulance in Italy.*

When the wrappings came off, 18-year-old Ernie Hemingway wondered whether the doctor would have to cut his leg off. There was so much sticky blood, so many cuts, his right kneecap down on his shin. A bit of irony, the writer in him might have said—he wasn't an infantryman. He was never meant to return from a battlefield with injuries of his own. His job was to save soldiers. Ernie Hemingway wasn't meant to lose *anything*.

As he lay on a stretcher in a first aid station on the Italian front, he could look back at his short life and all that had happened. A little over a year earlier, in April 1917, the United States had entered the Great War. Most of the fellows like him who graduated from high school in the leafy Chicago suburb of Oak Park wanted to get in on the war. Just kids, they had started their senior year never dreaming that they'd get the chance. At that point, Americans were not interested in fighting Europe's battles. But over the winter all that had changed, and the United States had declared war on Kaiser Bill's Germany and its ally, the Empire of Austria-Hungary—"Huns," the newspapers called them.

At Oak Park and River Forest High School, Ernie had enjoyed sports. He ran track and played a little football. He had liked his English classes as well and was proud that his teachers had named him an editor of the *Trapeze*, the school paper. He wrote short stories, imitating the style of Ring Lardner, the most popular author of the day. Ernie was just a kid, and he hadn't yet found his rhythm, his own way of storytelling. But Ernie Hemingway never doubted that he was going to be a writer.

First, however, Ernie wanted to be a soldier. But his father had other ideas. Dr. Clarence Hemingway refused to sign a form for Ernie to enlist, and without his dad's permission, the army wouldn't take him until six months after he turned 20. So things weren't going well at home. Once he graduated from high school, Ernie drove his parents crazy. He refused to do the respectable thing and go to college.

But his mother and father did agree to a compromise and let him leave home—under an uncle's watchful eye—to try his luck as a cub reporter for the *Kansas City Star*. Ernie adored that first job. He covered murders, fires, and a breakout of smallpox that gave him a chance to take an ambulance ride as he reported on the story.

Ernie's successful probationary period at the *Star* apparently impressed Dr. Hemingway, and he finally signed the form that allowed Ernie to enlist. Ernie started making plans to fight in France with General John Pershing's American Expeditionary Forces. Then disappointment came his way: though he'd never worn glasses, Ernie flunked the army physical because he couldn't pass the eye exam.

So Ernie, like lots of red-blooded American boys, took a different path to get in on the war. He signed up with the American Red Cross to drive ambulances on the Italian front. These Red Cross volunteers, mostly college men from Ivy League schools, hauled wounded soldiers from first aid stations at the front to field hospitals behind the lines of battle.

Short weeks later, Ernie sailed for France with an assortment of other young Americans who were looking for a thrill. Most had never believed they'd get to Europe at this point in their lives. Ernie got his first look at Paris as it was being shelled by German artillery, and then he headed south over the mountains to northern Italy.

Except for the handful of ambulance drivers working for the Red Cross, the Italian front was uncharted territory for Americans in that summer of 1918. Still, the drivers knew they faced danger. Several ambulance units had worked in France since 1914. Their casualty counts proved that big German cannons did not discriminate between healthy soldiers and wounded ones— or ambulance drivers who, after all, were unpaid volunteers.

Second Lieutenant Ernest Hemingway, American Red Cross, smartly uniformed with his dark hair slicked to one side, reported for duty at *Croce Rossa Americana* headquarters in Milan. He was ready for the challenge. Ambulance corpsmen drove two kinds of "machines":

Ernest Hemingway in uniform.
Ernest Hemingway Collection. John F. Kennedy Presidential Library and Museum, Boston.

decked-out Model T Fords for running along the Italian plains, and tougher Italian-made Fiats that could handle the demands of steep, rocky grades.

But the combat experience Ernie was hoping for didn't come. Things were quiet in Sector 4, the area where the Red Cross dispatched him. Ernie spent a few days at his new job and decided that it was boring. He craved action, and he went looking until he found some at Fossalta, a shelled wreck of a village that sat on the Piave River marking the line of battle between the Italian and Austrian armies. The Red Cross operated a *cucina* there, a field kitchen that offered fighting men a supply of hot coffee, chocolate bars, and cigarettes.

Ernie took up a new assignment, crawling in and out of trenches to hand out smokes and candy bars to Italian soldiers. He loved to talk, and he practiced speaking Italian with them. As he moved between the forward posts along the battle line, he could hear the boom of big guns firing from both sides and the whine of shells as they landed. Ernie Hemingway was living life and war as no Oak Parker could have imagined.

The Italian army was dug into trenches that ran for miles along the Piave River to Mount Grappa, a strategic spot that led north into the Alps. On the other side of no-man's-land, perhaps 50 yards away, Austro-Hungarian soldiers lived in trenches of their own. A few weeks before, the Italians had driven the Austrian invaders back across the Piave. For the time being, the Italians and Austrians were at a stalemate, dug into trenches and waiting for their commanders to call the next move. But no one could relax. Intermittent fire from field artillery kept soldiers on edge.

In the predawn hours of July 8, 1918, an Austrian howitzer fired a mortar across no-man's-land and into the trench occupied by Ernie and a group of Italians. The shell blew open and rained debris everywhere. Four men took the brunt of the attack. One died instantly, torn apart. The second had his legs blown away. The third was gravely injured. Ernie was bleeding from the knees down.

Broad shouldered and a strong six feet tall, Ernie hoisted up the injured Italian, put him on his back, and carried him to the rear of the battle line. As he unsteadily picked his way through a storm of machine gun bullets and artillery fire, he was hit in the right knee, "like a sharp smack on the leg with an icy snow ball," he wrote to his family. Down he went with the Italian on his back. Somehow—he would never understand how or why—he regained his footing and delivered the injured soldier to the first aid station. Then he passed out.

Or so the story went.

When Ernie regained consciousness, he was lying on a stretcher. Litter bearers had carried him three kilometers to a wound station. The Italians were still under attack, and Ernie's letter home was filled with the sights and sounds of the battle:

> [T]he road was having the "entrails" shelled out of it. Whenever a big one would come, Whee—whoosh—Boom—they'd lay me down and get flat. . . . The shelling was still pretty thick and our batteries were going off all the time way back of us and the big 250's and 350's [250- and 350-millimeter guns] going over head for Austria with a noise like a railway train.

Medics injected Ernie with painkilling morphine and an antitetanus serum, shaved his legs, and removed 28 pieces of shrapnel. He endured a five-day wait at a field hospital until the doctor said he could be moved to the Red Cross hospital in Milan.

Ernie's career with the Red Cross was over in only three weeks. It would take months before his legs would heal. He wrote that his wounds were the work of a single Austrian *Minenwerfer*, a five-gallon metal shell filled with "the goddamnedest collection of crap you ever saw—nuts, bolts, screws, nails, spikes, metal scrap."

"Shells aren't bad except direct hits," he said. "You must take chances on the fragments of the burst. But when there is a direct hit your pals get spattered all over you. Spattered is literal."

On July 21, 1918, Ernie celebrated his 19th birthday in the *Ospedale Americana* in Milan. The converted residence seemed as much a country club as hospital. Rooms in the old villa looked out onto a shaded veranda where patients were encouraged to rest on hot afternoons. There was plenty to eat. For a small bribe, the hospital porter would deliver a bottle of liquor—breaking the rules and annoying Miss Katherine DeLong, the hospital's strict, no-nonsense nursing supervisor. Practically everyone smoked, a soldier's right both in the trenches and in the hospital.

The patients' rooms opened one to the other, so the young occupants visited each other back and forth. Only Ernie, with one leg in a cast and the other bandaged up, was bedridden. The others, all Red Cross volunteers like himself, were there because they had come down with diseases such as dysentery, the bloody diarrhea that so many men picked up by drinking contaminated water. Other patients had the telltale yellow skin of hepatitis, inflammation of the liver. These included Ernie's next-door neighbor, Henry Villard, whose own eyes and skin had turned a sickly gold. Henry and scores of his Harvard classmates had dropped out of college to go to war. Like Ernie, Henry was a good writer, and he kept a diary of his weeks in the Italian hospital.

Through the open door, Henry watched the comings and goings as Ernie Hemingway held court from his bed. Ernie turned out to be the most popular patient in the hospital. Propped up with pillows and immobilized under snow white sheets, he would show off a dish on his nightstand filled with the metal shreds of shrapnel that doctors had picked out of his legs. Red Cross nurses—real, live, English-speaking women

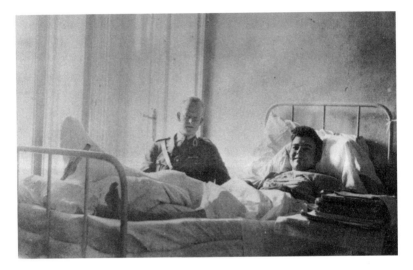

Henry Villard (seated) visits with Ernest Hemingway in the hospital.
Decades later he would put his memories on paper.
Ernest Hemingway Collection. John F. Kennedy Presidential Library and Museum, Boston

who, in theory, were forbidden to date their patients—dropped by to chat when they had a free moment. Italian officers came by as well. But most of the time Ernie kept company with other patients, fellows like him who had little to do during those long days in the hospital. Visitors loved Ernie's stories. He had a flair for language, and the more he told his tales, the bigger they grew.

Ernie often slipped a few lire to the porter who smuggled in bottles of vermouth or brandy, cognac or Cointreau. When Miss DeLong wasn't looking, he'd pull a liquor bottle from under his pillow and invite his visitors to take a swig. Henry Villard joined in for a drink once in a while, a bad choice for a jaundice patient with a sick liver. Ernie amazed Henry—young Hemingway could hold his booze like no one he'd ever seen, an "unlimited capacity to swallow the contents of a bottle without betraying the fact that he had been drinking."

In fact, Ernest Hemingway was becoming spoiled. His handsome face, capped by dark brown hair, his broad smile, and his larger-than-life personality drew people to him like flies to honey. Henry noticed that his new friend "Hem" could boss people around. More than one nurse left Hem's bedside thinking that he was uncooperative if not downright rude.

Ernest Hemingway, charming as he was, could be boorish and obnoxious. But Henry admired how Ernie could get away with bad behavior. Everyone knew how brave he'd been under fire. Not only that—Ernie still faced another surgery, and no one could be sure that he'd keep his right leg.

News from America arrived in dribs and drabs—more than once a ship carrying mail from home was sunk by the Germans. Like soldiers everywhere, Ernie and Henry followed baseball and liked to catch up on their home teams. Ernie liked the Chicago Cubs, who were having a fabulous season in 1918, while Henry followed the New York Giants and its hot-tempered manager, John J. McGraw. Even baseball had gone to war. Christy Mathewson, the former star pitcher for the Giants, had signed on with the Chemical Warfare Service.

Ernie and Henry also liked to play around with words. When war news trickled into the hospital, Hem or Henry liked to frame it like a sports story, running down reports from the front line as though they were box scores. To entertain themselves, Hem and Henry worked up a naughty bit of verse with a baseball theme that they kept under wraps:

Here lies the body of Mary Jones
For her life held no terrors;
She lived a maid and died a maid—
No hits, no runs, no errors.

From then on, "No hits, no runs, no errors" became their standard answer when anyone asked about their health.

Henry Villard and Ernie Hemingway had lots to talk about. Henry had taken his first trip to the American West the summer before, and Ernie eagerly listened to Henry's tales about galloping through sagebrush in the wide-open spaces. Ernie, though he'd never been west, was a first-rate outdoorsman. Every summer, the Hemingways decamped from Oak Park to their cabin in the pine woods of northern Michigan, where Dr. Hemingway taught his son how to bait a fish hook, handle a 12-gauge shotgun, and spend the night under the stars. Ernie rubbed elbows with people totally unlike the genteel citizens of Oak Park. Over the years he got well-acquainted with the locals— small-town Michiganders, ordinary farmers, and a handful of Ojibwa Indians. Back in high school, he'd published two short stories that he'd set in Michigan. He based the plots and characters on people he'd met there.

All during his months in Italy, Ernie soaked up his experiences. Though he didn't write them down, he never forgot what he saw and heard—tales of dark-caped soldiers retreating from death in the rain, machine guns going like riveters tat-a-tat tat-tat, the smell of blood, the throaty burn of Italian wine, and the feel of a woman in his arms.

Ernie Hemingway was falling in love with an American nurse. Lots of patients got crushes on the young women who took care of them, and of all the American and British women at the Red Cross Hospital, Agnes von Kurowsky was their favorite. The tall, pretty American with the German-sounding last name (though her father was Polish) hailed from Pennsylvania. "Fresh and pert and lively," thought Henry Villard, and he looked forward to taking Aggie out to dinner. Italian soldiers admired Aggie too, and she had the attentions of a blond-haired officer, Captain Enrico Serena, whose eye patch made him all the more intriguing.

It was against Red Cross rules for anyone to keep a diary, but Henry broke the rule, and busy as she was, Aggie kept one too.

She wrote a few lines every day, chatting about her duties, other nurses, her patients, and her boyfriend, the Italian officer. Life seemed very exciting to Aggie, who had worked as a librarian until she'd gone for nurse's training in New York. Aggie's diary had Italian headings at the top, and on "20 *Sabado*," Saturday, July 20, she noted:

> The Capt. walked home with me again & came in this time. He seemed delighted with our Hospital and took quite a fancy to Mr. Hemingway—who has the honor of being the 1st Amer. wounded in Italy. [In truth, an American Red Cross officer had been killed first, in June.] He has shrapnel in his knees, besides a great many flesh wounds.

The next night, Aggie wrote more about her patient, who was turning 19:

> 21 *Domenica* (Sunday)
> Mr. Hemingway's birthday, so we all dressed up, & had Gelati on the balcony & played the Victrola. Then Mr. Seely [another patient] brought him in a large bottle of 5 star Cognac, and they did make merry. I simply can't get to bed early these nights. Every night I start early, & get talking to someone & it's 12 before I know it.

Aggie von Kurowsky hadn't dated in several years, and now lots of men were paying attention to her. The Italian captain called on her almost daily, and she got a letter from a Belgian officer she'd met during her Atlantic crossing. "I have gone pretty far in the emotional pathway," she wrote. "Somehow, things you read about, never seem quite the same when they become one's own experience." Her Italian captain was far too intense—"he tells me how much he loves me, Yet when I say but I don't love you, it squelches him but a moment & then he begins again. And yet when he is not talking like that I like him very well."

Of course Ernie befriended the Italian officer, as he did nearly everyone who came to the *Ospedale Americana*. He "lectured" Aggie about her "meanness to the Capitano," which made her laugh. Then things changed. Captain Serena was making plans to move to Paris to do some family business, and Aggie decided to date other men.

Early on the morning of August 10, Ernie underwent his long-awaited surgery, the first operation to take place in the hospital. Both patients and staff watched the clock, wondering how it would go for their star patient. By afternoon, they could relax. "Everything went beautifully," Aggie wrote in her diary that night. "The Ital. doctor flashed smiles all around & learned a few Eng. Words such as 'needle—strong—enough.'"

Ernie Hemingway would keep his leg.

In her diary, Aggie went from writing about "Mr. Hemingway" to "Mr. H." to "the Kid" to "Ernie." Aggie was professional in her nursing duties and compassionate toward every young man she cared for, but she paid extra attention to Ernie. She worked the night shift, and when things were quiet among the sleeping patients she could slip into Ernie's room for a visit.

When she was off duty, another nurse carried notes back and forth between them, and Henry watched Hem and Aggie hold hands "in a manner that did not suggest she was taking his pulse." On August 25, Aggie wrote "Now, Ernest Hemingway has a case on me, or thinks he has. He is a dear boy & so cute about it. It does beat how popular I have become in the last 6 mos. Must be because I'm turning frivolous."

The next day she added, "Ernest Hemingway is getting earnest. He was talking last night of what might be if he was 26-28. In some way—at some times—I wish very much that he was. He is adorable & we are very congenial in every way. I'm getting

Agnes von Kurowsky and Ernest Hemingway.
Ernest Hemingway Collection. John F. Kennedy Presidential Library and Museum, Boston

so confused." Someone found one of her yellow hairpins under Ernie's pillow and the two went through no end of teasing.

When it came to men, Agnes von Kurowsky wasn't sure of herself. She kept up her relationship with Ernie, even as she'd call him "Kid" and tell him she was too old for him. The truth was that Ernie Hemingway, with his severe wounds and handsome boyish face, entranced her. For his part, Ernie never gave up on trying to win her heart. To him, age made no difference.

Ernie's romance with Aggie blossomed as the war went on around them. Patients and nurses came and went from the hospital, and Aggie learned she was being transferred to a new post. On October 15, she left for Florence. On October 24, Ernie got permission to go to the front and—well back of the action— watched some of the final battle between Italy and Austria at

Mount Grappa. From then on, Ernie liked to think he'd gone into battle there, alongside the elite Arditi, Italy's special forces who famously carried daggers in their teeth and fought to the death. The reality was that Ernie couldn't stand on his own two feet; he still leaned on a cane to help him manage his bum right leg.

Though he had watched men be blown apart in front of him, Ernie still felt invincible. He had faced death and survived. Serving in war still offered a challenge and a thrill, and Ernie planned to return to ambulance duty when released from the hospital. But that opportunity never came.

On November 11, 1918, the Armistice was signed in France, ending the war and stopping the shooting in Italy. Ernie was back in the hospital; somewhere he'd picked up hepatitis, and he was undergoing a round of physical therapy for his leg. He and Aggie carried on their romance by writing letters. They saw each other one last time on December 9, when Ernie visited Aggie in the mountain town of Treviso, where she nursed soldiers who were dying from Spanish flu. Ernie was full of himself, and his grandiose stories sent seasoned fighting men into gales of laughter. But Aggie was in love with him, and she agreed to get married once Ernie was home and making some money as a writer.

In January 1919, Ernie Hemingway came home to 600 North Kenilworth Avenue in Oak Park. News of his war experiences had arrived long before he did. His family thought he was a hero, and he got a hero's welcome from everyone else who had read articles in the village newspaper, the *Oak Leaves*. These were often blown way out of proportion, but Ernie never tried to set the record straight.

Oak Park High School invited him to make a speech, and Ernie conveniently set aside the ethics he'd learned as an impartial newspaperman. Shamelessly, he went on stage and became Ernest Hemingway the storyteller. He told about the daring Arditi, saying that they were condemned murderers who'd been released from prison in exchange for going on suicide missions. He let his listeners think that he'd gone into combat himself, spinning a tale about bleeding men who stuffed bullet holes with cigarettes and kept on fighting.

Ernie wore his uniform all around Oak Park, while other veterans had put theirs away in the attic. He gave speeches to admiring women's clubs, fired off souvenir star shells in the backyard, and pulled out daggers and helmets and medals to show off when his friends dropped by. His small brother wondered why Ernie put on this grand display only when company came.

Then Ernie got a letter from Aggie. On March 7, she wrote him a "Dear John" letter—which no soldier ever wanted to open—with news that she was breaking their engagement. Ernie was too young for her, she explained. "I can't get away from the fact that you're just a boy—a kid." And as a matter of fact, she added, she was engaged to marry someone else. Aggie wished him well, "And I hope & pray that after you have thought things out, you'll be able to forgive me & start a wonderful career & show what a man you really are."

The heady days of living in Italy and the excitement of falling in love were over for Ernie Hemingway. Aggie had left him for good. He didn't take the news well and wrote angry letters to his friends, telling one he hoped that Aggie would take a fall and break some teeth.

Then Ernie broke with his family over his plans to work as a writer. His parents, products of a duty-bound Victorian age, were proud that he had helped make the world safe for democracy and had come home in one piece. Dr. and Mrs. Hemingway could not understand why their son wouldn't do something useful like go to college or get a "real" job. In their view, sitting at a typewriter all day pounding out stories didn't count. All around, the fighting men of the Great War had come home to work, marry, settle down, and raise families—a return to "normalcy" that most people wanted in their lives. But Ernie Hemingway would never feel normal. He had an artist's soul and thought of himself as a writer, and he was serious about making himself a better one.

In his old bedroom, Ernie typed story after story and submitted them to popular magazines like the *Saturday Evening Post*. Ernie continued to imitate the writing styles of authors he admired even as he struggled to create a voice all his own. Most of his submissions came back with rejection slips. But it wasn't in Ernie's nature to give up, so he kept working and reworking his ideas, his observations, and his memories into words.

Eventually Ernie Hemingway bundled up his feelings for Aggie and moved on. He worked for a while as an aide and companion to a disabled man, reported for the *Toronto Star*, and wrote for a Chicago newspaper. In 1921 he married an older woman, Hadley Richardson, and they moved to Paris, where rent was cheap and artists were flocking. The City of Light drew young writers from the United States, Great Britain, and Ireland, all veterans of the Great War. Their names would appear on reading lists in high schools and colleges in years to come: James Joyce, John Dos Passos, Robert Graves, and e. e. cummings. Others who never made it into battle fit right in, including the up-and-coming novelist F. Scott Fitzgerald, along with his wife, Zelda. These men of letters drank and smoked and loved and wrote and tossed ideas around like kids playing ball— and Ernie flourished among them.

As he moved further into his 20s and time put distance between him and his months in Italy, Ernest Hemingway hit his stride as a writer. In 1928, he published *The Sun Also Rises*, a novel about hard-living American expatriates who, like him, vacationed in Spain to watch the running of the bulls. He opened his tale with a comment passed on to him by Gertrude Stein, an older, plain-speaking art critic who'd also driven ambulances in France. "You are all a lost generation," she had told him. He denied it, calling the idea "bullshit," but it did make for a good story.

Three years later Ernest Hemingway published his master-piece, *A Farewell to Arms*. He set his novel about the Great War in Italy, telling the tale of a bitter, disillusioned ambulance driver, Frederic Henry, who deserts the army and surprises himself by falling in love with a nurse. It took him half a year to write the first draft, but when he'd finished, he knew he'd created some-thing special. More antihero than hero, Frederic Henry's char-acter reflects Ernest Hemingway's own search for what it means to be a man who loses love and lives in a world where he has no control.

Was he writing about Aggie and himself? Of course—to a point. But as Ernest always insisted, his stories and his charac-ters grew out of a mix of his own experiences, other peoples' lives, the stories he'd heard, and what he simply made up. His writing became known for what was not there, the "iceberg the-ory," some critics called it; Hemingway's spare words left much underneath for his readers to think about. The young Ernie might have used words like lavish embroidery to decorate the truth, but Ernest Hemingway the man found no need to do so.

Ernest Hemingway went on to become one of the 20th cen-tury's leading authors. He challenged himself to live a rugged, macho life as a man's man. He hunted big game, skied steep mountains, adored deep sea fishing, drank hard, chased women, and married four times. When wars came, he returned to his old role as a reporter at the scene of the action, first in Spain during the Spanish Civil War, then to cover Japan's invasion of China in 1937, and again reporting from Europe during World War II.

He always struggled to find in himself another story to tell, another book to write. In 1940 he published the wildly success-ful *For Whom the Bell Tolls* about the Spanish Civil War, and in 1952 he published a small jewel, *The Old Man and the Sea*, which earned him the Pulitzer Prize. The Nobel Prize for Literature became his in 1954, the ultimate recognition for his life's work.

Hemingway's own life ran like a thread through his books. Decade by decade, the main characters in his novels, always men, grew older just as the author himself aged. He gave his characters bleak lives and a sense of desolation, as if something they craved were forever out of reach. Then "Papa," as his friends knew him, began to display the same emptiness. He plummeted into long months of depression and became a worry to his wife, sons, and friends. "Black-Ass," he called his dark moods.

Gertrude Stein may well have been correct that Ernest Hemingway was "lost." Some would say that he had begun his journey of quiet desperation at the Italian front in 1918. He had overcome undeniably tough challenges, yet it seemed that he spent his life searching for something he could never find. In the end, his outward success as a novelist meant nothing. Sick, depressed, and convinced that the writer in him could no longer find the words he needed, Ernest Hemingway died by his own hand in 1961. His weapon of choice was a shotgun.

THE CAPTAIN

★ ★ ★

HARRY TRUMAN

> Harry S. Truman (1884–1972) served as an artillery officer in the Great War and went on to become the 33rd president of the United States in 1945.

In the summer of 1918, a young woman named Elizabeth Wallace of Grandview, Missouri, watched and waited for letters coming from France. She was like hundreds of thousands of wives, mothers, sisters, and girlfriends whose men were overseas fighting with General Pershing's American Expeditionary Forces. Bess, as she was called by her family and friends, wrote faithfully to her Harry, and she was a lucky girl, because her beau, a farmer-turned-soldier named Harry Truman, enjoyed writing letters, too.

Harry had adored Bess ever since they'd met at Sunday school in the First Presbyterian Church of Independence, Missouri. They were in the same class, Harry born in May 1884 and Bess the following February. They went to school together in

Independence, the county seat of a farming community east of Kansas City in northwest Missouri.

Bess could hold her own with the rough-and-tumble boys at school; she was "the first girl I ever knew who could whistle through her teeth and bat a ball as far as any boy in the neighborhood," said an admirer. Unlike those boys at school, Harry played the piano—so well that his teachers had hopes that one day he'd be a concert pianist. He was a bookish lad who pored over histories thick with tales of inspiring generals like Hannibal, Alexander the Great, Julius Caesar, Napoleon, George Washington, and Robert E. Lee. To read them, he wore a pair of thick glasses that earned him the nickname Four-Eyes.

Harry was "blind as a stump," folks would say, and when he turned 21 and became a legal adult, he memorized the eye chart to make sure he could sign up for the National Guard in Kansas City and pass his military physical. He joined Battery B, an artillery unit tasked with firing the big guns whose shells could fly for miles into enemy territory. This kind of warfare demanded soldiers who were good at math and understood geometry, so Harry, known for his numbers skills as a bookkeeper in a bank, was handpicked for the job. He spent six years in the Missouri Guard, first as a private and then as a corporal from 1905 until 1911.

By then Harry had moved back to the Truman family farm in Grandview, 10 miles south of Independence. His father had fallen on hard times, and with the family facing financial ruin, Harry did the honorable thing and left the bank to work the farm. At 600 acres, it was nearly a square mile of land to manage. From Grandview it was a much longer trip to training with his guard unit, not to mention that it was farther from Bess. He had his eye on her, that pretty girl with "tanned skin[,] blond hair, golden as sunshine, and the most beautiful blue eyes I've ever seen or ever will see." True to form, the loyal Harry kept close to several friends in Battery B. He regretted he couldn't rejoin his unit when it went with General John Pershing to New Mexico in 1916 to chase down the Mexican bandit Pancho Villa.

In 1910 Harry began courting Bess in earnest. Her mother didn't approve of the match: Harry wasn't in the same social circle as the Wallaces. Bess, along with her brothers and their snobbish mother, had moved into her grandparents' Independence home following her father's death. They were city people who attended the high-end Episcopalian church and sat down to the dinner table in the evening.

By contrast, Harry and all the others in Grandview kept to farmers' hours, eating their big meal at noon with a lighter supper in the evening. Harry tried to see Bess on weekends—it was a 16-mile trip by buggy into Independence—and he earnestly courted her by writing scores of letters with chatty but forthright observations about himself, life on the farm, human nature, and his own plans to become successful and prosperous in business, mining, or maybe politics.

Bess first turned Harry down when he proposed marriage via a letter he sent in 1911, and it took Harry another two years and many more letters until he got his wish. Bess told him in a backhanded way that "ever if she married anyone it would be him," and they became secretly engaged. For years, Harry tried his hand as a businessman and miner, and he learned that making easy money wasn't among his talents. He couldn't afford an engagement ring, much less provide a home for Bess.

They still hadn't married when the United States declared war on Germany and entered World War I in April 1917 as allies of France and Great Britain. As far back as 1914, Harry had thought that "when Germany invaded Belgium, my sympathies were all on the side of France and England. . . . I rather felt we owed France something for Lafayette."

Late in June 1918, Harry Truman rejoined the Missouri National Guard, now a full-sized artillery regiment. He was assigned to Battery F of the 2nd Missouri Field Artillery

Regiment. To his great surprise, his fellow soldiers elected him as a first lieutenant (National Guard officers were elected rather than appointed in those days). He recruited others to sign up, and with the zest he was known for, he drilled and developed them into soldiers. On the Fourth of July, they paraded through a park in Kansas City, and later that day, Harry appeared on Bess's front porch dressed in his new uniform complete with cap, riding crop, and silver spurs.

Bess, still living in Independence with her mother, would wait years to marry her "young man." The truth was, Harry wasn't young anymore. He was 33, well past the age limit for the army to draft men into service. She wanted to get married before he left for France, but Harry didn't want his darling Bess to be left a widow if he were killed. Wedding plans were put on hold.

One month later, the US Army called up the National Guard into service, and Harry's regiment took its new name: the 129th Field Artillery, United States Army. Harry passed another physical; his trusty glasses corrected his vision to 20/23 and 20/40, acceptable to army standards. In late September, Batteries D and F rolled out of Kansas City on railway cars headed to Camp Doniphan, a brand-new training site in Oklahoma. Harry brought his red 1911 Stafford touring car. The regiment had few gasoline vehicles—in those days, the army still relied on horses to pull its cannons and other heavy artillery. Harry's car, wildly popular with everyone, went into service 24/7 until he left for France in March 1918. Then he sold it for $200.

Harry Truman never worked harder in his life than he did during the first month of artillery training at camp near Chaumont. Learning how to effectively shoot a heavy cannon or light artillery demanded highly technical skills that Harry hadn't yet learned. He'd never gone to college, and now he was called on to study math-heavy surveying and astronomy, which turned out to be much more a numbers game than mere stargazing.

Harry reprogrammed his brain to think in the metric system—the training manuals for those French 75s he was firing were plotted in meters and not in feet or yards. The French prized their "marvel weapon." Artillerymen firing the 75mm field gun could get off as many as 20 to 30 shots per minute, delivering shells filled with explosives or gas as far as five miles distant. Even at 3,000 pounds, atop its own horse-pulled carriage, the gun was considered to be easy to move. Battery D had four French 75s, and "the fire from a battery of four was murderous."

Whenever he had a spare moment, Harry wrote letters home. Usually a month passed before they'd arrive, and invariably, several showed up in the mail at once. As newsy as ever, Harry chronicled the ins and outs of training as well as his take on the lovely sights in France.

He talked about his progress as an officer—as first lieutenant and then a training captain.

Angers France
June 19, 1918

Dear Bess:
This is the grandest afternoon I've spent since I've been in France. I received seven, count 'em, seven letters from you, five from Mary [Harry's sister]. . . . I saved yours until last because I wanted the most possible enjoyment and worked things on a climax basis. You've no idea what a grand and glorious feeling it is to have seven letters from the only girl in the world poked at you by a mail orderly.

Harry caught up with Battery D early in July at Camp Coëtquidan, the unit's last stop for training before going to the front. His boss shocked him by announcing that Harry was now commander of Battery D of the 129th Regiment. He was in charge of four big guns, 188 men, 167 horses, and everything that came with them, from artillery shells for the guns to hay for the horses.

Harry had been handed the orneriest unit of uncooperative men among the six batteries of the 129th. Several commanders had already come and gone. He called his men to order for his first meeting as commander, and when they laid eyes on their new captain, the old-looking guy with a pair of pince-nez glasses perched on his nose, they took him to be a fool. Harry gave a slow, full inspection without saying a word. Once he dismissed them and turned away, the soldiers puffed up their cheeks, stuck their tongues through their lips, and gave him a Bronx cheer. The insult was loud and clear.

The next morning, a revised personnel list was pinned to the announcement board. Captain Truman had busted several sergeants—noncommissioned officers who were supposed to keep the enlisted men in line—back to private. For the time being, he had no more trouble from his soldiers. Several battles later, his men would think the world of him.

For a month Harry worked like a fiend with the men of Battery D, transforming them from probably the worst to the finest artillery battery in the 129th. Harry called them the "Irish." Made up of a tough bunch of working-class Irish and German Catholics, mostly high school grads and a few college men from Kansas City, the unit became known as "Dizzy D." Harry, a Protestant, made it a point to get to know them personally, and he made sure their rations improved. Reading all those history books had taught him that an army moves on its belly.

Harry's letters home to Bess traced the progress of Battery D all through August, September, October, and November of 1918, the final four months of a four-year war. He was frank enough in what he said, but of course Harry left out the precise details of each battle and what he and his men faced under fire. As a captain, Harry knew better than to write anything too specific.

Though he never went to college, Harry Truman was an ardent student of history.
Harry S. Truman Presidential Library and Museum

After all, he was obliged to censor the letters of the men he commanded. He'd be remiss to make the same mistake; still, his superiors marked up and deleted some of what he wrote to Bess and the rest of his family.

For its first foray into battle, Battery D was dispatched to the southernmost end of the Western Front in the Alsace region, where the fighting was not as fierce as farther north. Battery D proved to be a model of efficiency, loading 17 flatcars and 30 French boxcars with men, guns, gun carriages, field kitchens, horses, documents, and more in 48 minutes flat. The enlisted men rode in the boxcars marked *40 Hommes 8 Cheveuax* (40 Men 8 Horses). Along with his officers, Harry rode in a lone passenger coach, writing later to Bess that he missed the bigger, better fitted Pullman railway cars of home. Except for short stops (the men weren't permitted to get off the boxcars), it was a two-day journey to their destination, the Vosges Mountains. A huge Allied encampment sat on one side of a valley. A mile and a half away sat the heavily entrenched Germans.

Led by Captain Harry Truman, the men, horses, and guns of Battery D started a steep climb into the woods. Harry had chosen a spot for their field guns at the tree line some 2,000 feet higher than camp. They had just settled in when an order came for them to move one mile nearer to the Germans to fire their first barrage, shells filled with poison gas. They moved, and at 8:00 PM on August 29, 1918, Battery D let loose with 500 rounds.

Somewhere in Parle Vous
September 1, 1918

Dear Bess:
I am the most pleased person in the world this morning. I got two letters from you and have accomplished my greatest wish. Have fired five hundred rounds at the Germans at my command, been shelled, didn't run away thank the Lord, and never lost a man. Probably shouldn't have told you but you'll not worry any more if you know I'm in it than if you think I am. Have had the most strenuous week of my life, am very tired but otherwise absolutely in good condition physically, mentally, and morally.

It has been about two weeks since I've written you because I haven't had the chance. They shipped me from school to the front in charge of Battery D and the Irish seem to be pleased over it. We went into position right away and fired five hundred rounds at them in thirty-six minutes. Two of my guns got stuck in the mud, it was dark and raining, and before I could get away bing came the reply. I sent two of the pieces to safety, the horses on the other two broke away and ran every which direction but my Irishmen stayed with me, except a few drivers who were badly scared and my first sergeant. . . .

My greatest satisfaction is that my legs didn't succeed in carrying me away, although they were very anxious to do it. Both of my lieutenants are all wool and a yard wide. One of them, Jordon by name, came back with the horses off the other two pieces [guns] to pull me out, and I had to order him off the hill. Four horses were killed, two of them outright and two had to be shot afterwards.

Harry didn't write Bess the full details of Battery D's first experience under fire, which nearly ended in disaster. The whole truth came out later, in memoirs and official histories of the 129th Field Artillery. Fearing the Germans would fire gas back at them, the men were wearing gas masks. They were preparing to move and waiting for the first sergeant to bring up the horses when the Germans fired back—with artillery, not gas—and all hell broke loose. Harry, commanding on horseback, was thrown into a hole, his horse on top of him. Two of the guns, pulled by panicked horses, rolled over a hill and got stuck in the mud. The first sergeant and most of the soldiers panicked and ran too. It was dark and raining hard.

Harry shouted at his men with verbiage of his own, pulling out every curse and dirty word he'd heard in his 34 years. Shocked at his fury—they hadn't expected proper, bespectacled Captain Truman to muster up such foul language—his men came to their senses. They regrouped and Harry ordered them to march back downhill. The next day, he and a few others made the trip back up the mountain to rescue their guns and what horses were still alive. He demoted his first sergeant to private and had him transferred.

Harry Truman had won his men's respect.

After a two-day march out of the valley, they piled back on railroad cars headed for a battlefield farther north. Battery D detrained to rest a bit, and Harry fired off another letter to Bess.

Sept 8 1918

Dear Bess:
. . . I think I am the luckiest person in the world to be here and if I can deliver the goods and come out all right it will be the greatest honor a man can have. If I don't deliver, I'll have failed trying my level best and that's all any man can do.

> *As I told you before there isn't a German shell made for me. I think that my battery and myself will come through all safe and sound. We have had one brush as I told you and came out very very lucky. If I get sent home now they can't take away the satisfaction that I unloaded some very effective ammunition at the Boches and from what I can gather, I must have hit the target. . . . The men think I am not much afraid of shells but they don't know. I was too scared to run and that is pretty scared.*

On September 10 Battery D marched over two nights through the rain toward St. Mihiel, where Harry's unit was held in reserve, battle ready. Harry's letter to Bess on September 15 spoke of his pride in his guns, which an inspector had deemed "in the best condition of any in France," and in his men. "I am plumb crazy about my Battery. They sure step when I ask them to. We had to get ready for a night march a day or two ago and my bunch beat the regiment by nearly a half hour."

Harry Truman had a knack for sizing up his men and building on their talents—artillery training, horsemanship, kitchen duty, and supply work. Harry had grasped the very essence of a good manager. Whether he sat in a tidy office in Kansas City or in the mud in France, he knew how to run an organization.

> I sit back and inform them (the lieutenants) and my sergeants what I want done, and it is. My noncoms, now, are whizzes. I sorted 'em over, busted a lot and made a lot. They've gotten so they don't know whether to trust my smile or not, because I smile when I bust 'em and the same when I make 'em.

Battery D didn't fire a shot at St. Mihiel, but the next few days put the men to the test when they were forced to march north. The Allied Supreme Command had new plans, "a colossal, all-out offensive to end the war." French, British, and American forces massed along the full length of the Western Front, the Americans assigned a 24-mile stretch from the Meuse River to the Argonne Forest. Historians would record it as the Battles of the Meuse-Argonne, which dragged on from September 26 until the war ended.

For a week in the mud and rain—traveling at night to keep the Germans from spotting their movements—marched Harry, his men, their guns, and their horses. They hurried as best they could to arrive on time at Hill 290, a half mile from the small village of Neuvilly near the Belgian border. The soldiers carried 70-pound packs; the horses worked overtime pulling gun carriages through the muck. Exhausted, the slow-moving column of men and beasts slept under the cover of trees during the day. In the end, the forced march worked, and on September 23 at 3:00 AM they arrived. For three days, Battery D prepared for battle, 188 men among the 600,000 Americans swarming the Western Front to hurl everything they had at the German army.

At 4:20 AM on September 26, 1918, Battery D moved into action, one four-gun unit among 2,700 in all. The entire American line lit up with fire, the bombardment so loud that men were deafened for days. According to plan, each battery was to fire 1,000 rounds per hour at the barbed wire forest draped across no-man's-land, taking turns so the guns could cool down for 10 minutes every hour.

At 5:20, Battery D moved forward in a rolling barrage first of artillery fire aimed to land just ahead of the American infantry as it moved forward toward the German line. The far side of no-man's-land lay one and a half miles away, and the battle plan called for the Americans to move at a pace of 100 meters every four minutes. Reality proved otherwise, and what should have been a six- or seven-hour assault lasted 12 hours into the night.

At first light, Harry and his men were back on the march, now bearing witness to the American dead the Germans had mowed down the day before. In the afternoon they arrived at a peach orchard, their destination, and Harry and a few others climbed a hill to set up an observation post. Battery D, of the 35th Division, was assigned to a sector with strict instructions to fire north.

Then, to the west, an American flare lit up the sky. Harry clearly saw a German gun battery on the move, no doubt preparing to fire on the Americans of the 28th Division west of him. He watched as the Germans and their horses pulled the guns into place. Harry bided his time until the horses were unhitched and led away. With pencil and paper he ran the numbers, and he sent his firing data back to his own gunners with orders to fire at will. They destroyed the German battery before it could attack.

Harry had disobeyed orders. Battery D was only to shoot within its own sector to the north, and he had fired westward. Harry faced court-martial, as his livid colonel reminded him when he chewed him out, but then the matter was dropped. He'd saved American lives. Years later, grateful veterans of the 28th Division would enter voting booths and cast their ballots for the captain in the 35th named Harry Truman.

For the next three days, September 28, 29, and 30, Battery D kept rolling as the 35th Division—and then the 1st Division that relieved it—pressed forward.

On October 2, Battery D was ordered back from the front to take a break from the fighting.

October 6, 1918

Dear Bess:
. . . . The great drive has taken place and I had a part in it, a very small one but nevertheless a part. The experience has been one that I can never forget. . . . The papers are in the street now saying that the Central Powers have asked for peace, and I was in the drive that did it! I shot out a German Battery, shot up his big observation post, and ruined another Battery when it was

moving down the road. . . . I brought my Battery forward under fire and never lost a horse nor a man. Had shells fall on all sides and I am as sure as I am sitting here that the Lord was and is with me. . . .

If this peace talk is true and we do get to come home soon, I can tell you a lot of things I can't write down. You will probably hear more than you wish.

In his next letter, Harry recapped old news, and he added new observations about America's infantrymen, the foot soldiers who did the lion's share of the fighting. Just as Lieutenant Ronald Tolkien offered high praise for the British Tommies, so did Captain Harry Truman for the American doughboys. In Harry's view, the men in the air corps had things easy (though Fred Libby or Quentin Roosevelt might have disagreed).

France October 8, 1918

Dear Bess:
. . . There were some three or four weeks from September 10 to October 6 that I did nothing but march at night and shoot or sleep in daylight. . . .

The heroes are all in the infantry. When a man goes up with them he really does something. We are only their supporters and don't get much real action. The easiest and safest place for a man to get is in the air service. They fly around a couple of hours a day, sleep in a featherbed every night, eat hotcakes and maple syrup for breakfast, pie and roast beef for supper every day, spend their vacations in Paris or wherever else it suits their fancy, and draw 20 percent extra pay for doing it. Their death rate is about like the quartermaster and ordnance departments and on top of it all they are dubbed the heroes of the war. Don't believe it, the infantry—our infantry—are the heroes of the war. There's nothing—machine guns, artillery, rifles, bayonets, mines, or anything else—that can stop them when they start. If we could keep up with them, they'd go to the Rhine in one swoop. . . .

Harry's next letter came from Vigneulles, a French village where Battery D was resting. As pretty as the countryside was, Harry discovered that getting along with the locals took both patience and cash.

France Oct 11 18

Dear Bess:
. . . You undoubtedly are right in giving me the dickens for not writing oftener but my duties have been so strenuous and my work so hard in the last two months that I have hardly had a minute to call my own. . . .
When we go anywhere to dine out over here we carry both bread and sugar. Sometimes we forget it and then it is necessary to use all our arts and wiles to persuade the proprietor of the place to let us have some. . . . These people love francs better than their country and they are extracting just as many of them from us as they possibly can. . . . You can always tell a French village by day or night, even if you can't see anything. They are very beautiful to stand off and look at, nestling down in pretty little valleys, as they always do, with red roofs and a church spire. But when you arrive there are narrow dirty streets and a malodorous atmosphere that makes you want to go back to the hill and take out your visit in scenery.

The Battles of the Meuse-Argonne raged on. On October 15, Harry and Battery D moved into place in the Sommedieue Sector, a battle region east of Verdun on the Meuse Heights. Verdun itself lay in ruins, a stark, bombed-out town that had given its name to a battle fought two years before when 400,000 French soldiers and roughly the same number of German soldiers died. Harry's men knew this was a really big show. It would be 19 days until Harry could write another letter, but somehow, in the midst of battle and shelling night after night, he sent a telegram to Bess (and the telegraph operator got his middle initial wrong).

Well and happy writing;
Harry T. Truman
Oct 19

The next day, Harry managed to get out a letter.

Oct 20 1918

Dear Bess:
This is certainly a banner day. I received four letters from you. . . . That was a very tame affair compared with what we have been through since as I told you in my last letters. I am awfully sorry I could not write to you in all that last time but it was simply an impossibility. For one thing I had nothing to write with and another I could not have written a sane coherent letter if I had tried. It was the most terrific experience of my life and I hope I don't have to go through with it many more times although we are going to bust Heine [the Germans] if it takes us all and I don't think there is a man in the organization who wouldn't give his life to do it. . . . We marched half across France and were at it every night. I lost nearly all my horses just from marching so far without getting enough rest. . . .
I haven't taken any unnecessary chances but I had to go back after my guns. No good battery commander would send anyone else after guns he'd left in position under the same circumstances I left those two. I don't claim to be a good B.C. [Battery Commander] but I have to act like one anyway. . . . It really doesn't seem possible that a common old farmer boy could take

*a battery in and shoot it on such a drive and I sometimes think
I just dreamed it.*

When he next had a moment to write Bess, Harry shared
how he'd improved as a commander. His letters increasingly
showed his disgust for the German emperor.

October 30, 1918

Dear Bess:
*. . . We sit around these Battery positions and wait for some-
thing to shoot at and make maps and do so many things that
are necessary and a lot that are not that I sometimes don't know
straight up from crossways. You know the Battery commander
is the man to whom "the buck" is passed both going up and
coming down, and he's got to watch his P's and Q's mighty
smartly if they don't succeed in getting something on him. . . .*
   *I was in the most famous war town [Verdun] in France
today. . . . I've never seen a more desolate sight. Trees that were
once most beautiful forest trees are stumps with naked branches
sticking out making them look like ghosts. The ground is simply
one mass of shell holes. . . .*
   *When the moon rises behind those tree trunks I spoke of
awhile ago you can imagine that the ghosts of the half-million
Frenchmen who were slaughtered here are holding a sorrow-
ful parade over the ruins. It makes you hope that His Satanic
Majesty has a particularly hot poker and warm corner for Bill
Hohenzollern [Kaiser Wilhelm II] when his turn comes to be
judged and found wanting. . . .*
   *I am just as homesick to see you as you can possibly be to see
me. I hope the time is short when we'll see each other. I love you
more and more and shall continue to be*
      Yours always
      Harry

This picture shows the utter devastation Harry writes of in his letters to Bess. *Copyright unknown, courtesy of Harry S. Truman Library and Museum*

The next day Harry shared another facet of war.

Nov 1 1918

Dear Bess:
I have just finished putting 1,800 shells over on the Germans in the last five hours. . . . One of their aviators fell right behind my Battery yesterday and sprained his ankle, busted up the machine, and got completely picked by the French and Americans in the neighborhood. They even tried to take their (there were two in the machine) coats. One of our officers, I am ashamed to say, took the boots off of the one with the sprained ankle and kept them.

The French, and Americans too for that matter, are souvenir crazy. If a guard had not been placed over the machine, I don't doubt that it would have been carried away bit by bit. . . . It is a great thing to swell your chest out and fight for a principle but it gets almighty tiresome sometimes. I heard a Frenchman remark that Germany was fighting for territory, England for the sea, France for patriotism, and Americans for souvenirs. Yesterday made me think he was about right. . . .

I think the green pastures of Grand Old Missouri are the best looking of any that I have seen in this world yet and I've seen several brands. The outlook I have now is a rather dreary one. There are Frenchmen buried in my front yard and Huns in the back yard and both litter up the landscape as far as you can see. Every time a Boche shell hits in a field over west of here it digs up a piece of someone. It is well I'm not troubled by spooks. . . .

By November 5 rumors flew that Kaiser Wilhelm had abdicated his throne and that Germany was about to surrender. But the fighting went on. Battery D remained under fire and got off more of its own as the Allies kept driving the Germans farther and farther back. Then, on the morning of November 11, Captain Truman handed a sergeant a note with an order to read it to his men. There were a few last barrages to fire, the final one at 10:45 AM. Harry had begun to write to Bess about 15 minutes earlier. His unusually graphic letter was filled with hate for the Germans.

This is probably the photo of Bess Wallace that Harry Truman carried in his uniform pocket.
Harry S. Truman Library and Museum

Nov. 11. 1918

Dear Bess:
*. . . We are all wondering what the Hun is going to do. . . . We
don't care what he does. He's licked either way he goes. . . . It's a
shame we can't go in and devastate Germany and cut off a few
of the Dutch kids' hands and feet and scalp a few of their old
men but I guess it will be better to make them work for France
and Belgium for fifty years.*

*I just got official notice that hostilities would cease at eleven
o'clock. . . . I knew that Germany could not stand the gaff. For
all their preparedness and swashbuckling talk they cannot
stand adversity. France was whipped for four years and never
gave up and one good licking suffices for Germany. . . .*

Here's hoping to see you soon.

Precisely at 11:00 AM on the 11th day of the 11th month of
1918, the Allies and Germans signed the Armistice in a railroad
car in a forest at Compiègne, France, and the fighting stopped.

When Harry wrote to Bess on November 15, he again praised
his men. "I wouldn't trade off the 'orneriest' one I've got for any
other whole Battery," he told her. "You know I have succeeded
in doing what it was my greatest ambition to do at the beginning of the war. That is to take a Battery through as Battery
commander and not lose a man."

Sometime after November 23 Bess received Harry's longest
letter yet. The censors were no longer cutting as many holes,
and Harry took full advantage to write a 25-page missive. Five
months would pass until he sailed for home, but on May 3, 1919,
he got his wish and rode in a soldiers' homecoming parade in
Kansas City.

Harry and Bess were married on June 28, 1919. With an old
friend from the National Guard, Harry went into the haberdash-
ery business, selling men's clothing and undergarments. Times

President Harry Truman and First Lady Bess Truman share smiles at the Army-Navy football game in 1948. *Harry S. Truman Library and Museum*

were tough, and Truman & Jacobson soon went out of business. In 1922 Harry entered county politics as a Democrat. Moving upward as he got to know folks across the state, the likeable Harry was elected junior senator from Missouri in 1934. During his second senate term, Harry was picked to run as President Franklin Delano Roosevelt's vice president in the 1944 national election. The Democrats held onto the White House that year; the United States was in the midst of fighting World War II.

As the war drew to a close, FDR's health deteriorated rapidly, and on the morning of April 12, 1945, he died at his Georgia retreat. Harry Truman, the farm boy and underwear salesman from Missouri, was sworn in as president of the United States.

His first four months in office posed challenges that would have overwhelmed a lesser man. Harry Truman oversaw the

Allied victory against Germany and Japan, culminated by his—
and only his—decision to drop two atomic bombs on Japan in
order to end the war and ultimately spare the lives of 500,000
American soldiers.

The debate still rages about whether that decision was correct. Harry Truman, an eyewitness to war's devastation, took
full responsibility. He'd written Bess long ago that he, Battery
D's commander, was "the man to whom 'the buck' is passed
both going up and coming down." As president, Harry Truman
would forever insist that, at his desk in the Oval Office, "the
buck stops here."

THE COMEDIAN

* * *

BUSTER KEATON

Buster Keaton (1895–1966) was already an American vaude-ville star when he reported for duty as an ordinary soldier. He was just getting a start in movies in Hollywood's very youngest days when his draft notice arrived.

The US Army caught up with Buster Keaton in the summer of 1918. There it was, one among 24 million draft registration cards issued to American men. Buster had plenty of stage savvy as the youngest member of the Three Keatons, a vaudeville act that toured the United States, coast to coast. But no amount of smarts would get him out of serving in the army, even if he'd wanted to try.

Born Joseph Frank Keaton IV, he joined his parents, Joe and Myra, on stage at the age of three. The family went on to add the younger children, Harry and Louise, to the act, which Joe called "The Man with a Wife, Table, and Three Kids." Vaudeville was wildly popular among Americans, who flocked to theaters where singers, musicians, and comedians made them laugh.

Small and bouncy, Buster had earned his nickname after falling down a set of tall stairs in a boarding house when he was just learning to walk. The little boy learned how to take a fall without getting hurt and quickly became his father's favorite onstage prop. Joe Keaton's broad physical comedy—slapstick—got the most laughs when he heaved Buster up by a suitcase handle strapped under his clothes and tossed his son across the stage or through a backdrop. Buster became Joe Keaton's "human mop," and Buster's father would literally wipe the stage with his son. Modern audiences would regard this act as child abuse, but audiences in the early 1900s didn't see things that way.

As the Three Keatons perfected their routine—Joe tossing Buster, and Buster's mother blasting away on her saxophone—they played to bigger and better houses. When they got to New York, the prize destination for performers of all stripes, Joe got in trouble with the law for putting an underage child on stage. He blithely added two years to Buster's age and sent him onstage anyway. In the end, the police prevailed, and the Keatons' act was banished from New York.

Buster walked away from the act in 1917. He was 21. Joe Keaton, an alcoholic, grew ever more depressed, and Buster tired of his father's increasing anger and instability. He moved to New York and was set to take a Broadway role when he was lured away to play a bit part in a film starring the 280-pound comic genius Roscoe "Fatty" Arbuckle. Arbuckle was as generous as he was gigantic and took on Buster as his protégé and understudy.

Buster moved to Hollywood and learned everything he could about the movie business, from dodging flying custard pies to staging sight gags, a hallmark of the early days of silent flicks. At a young age, Buster had learned to get the biggest laughs by showing absolutely no expression after taking a hard fall. "Deadpan," showbiz folks tagged his hangdog look, and forevermore Buster Keaton reigned as the Great Stone Face of American comedy.

But his stage and screen career was interrupted in June 1917 when he was called to serve in the war.

Buster's draft notice ordered him to report to Camp Kearney, home to California's 40th Division, 159th Infantry, Company C, on July 24, 1918. His income dropped from the $250 a week he earned as an actor to $30, basic pay for an army private. At five foot four inches tall in his stocking feet, he didn't fill out even the smallest army uniform. He looked and felt like a clown. Worse, he was issued size-eight shoes for his size-six-and-a-half feet. Buster was destined to spend the rest of the war slapping around in those army shoes, "hobnailed and made of leather as tough as a rhinoceros's hide."

Private Keaton had his doubts about his army service.

It was not always possible to take that war seriously. In the first place I could not understand why we, the French, and English were fighting the Germans and the Austrians. Being in vaudeville all of my life had made me international-minded. I had met too many kindly German performers—singers and acrobats and musicians—to believe they could be as evil as they were being portrayed in our newspapers. Having known Germans, Japanese jugglers, Chinese magicians, Italian tenors, Swiss yodelers and bell-ringers, Irish, Jewish, and Dutch comedians, British dancers, and whirling dervishes from India, I believed people from everywhere in the world were about the same. Not as individuals, of course, but taken as a group.

With only two weeks of training at home, Company C shipped out by rail to Camp Upton in Long Island, New York,

The Great Stone Face poses
in his doughboy uniform
after the war.
*The California State
Military Museum*

the final stop for most
doughboys before head-
ing to France. Buster was
happy to make this stop,
since his girl Natalie lived
not far off. The gifted master of illusion managed an
illegal date off post by posing as an officer, saluting
watchful sentries as he rode
past in Natalie's chauffeur-
driven Packard.

Buster shipped out to France, and every night for the seven
months he spent there, he slept on the ground or floor in mills,
barns, and stables. He caught a bad head cold that went into his
ears, and within a month, his officers had to shout their orders
to him. Nevertheless, Buster played the quiet rebel as often as
he could.

In that war we saw little but rain and mud. But this is
not the reason I recall so clearly the first day that the
sun shone. I found some blackberries along a road that
afternoon, and climbed up on a low stone wall to pick
them. While bending over I became aware that someone
was behind me. Looking through my legs I could see the
leather puttees [leggings] of an officer and the end of his
little swagger stick.

I straightened up, turned around, and came to attention. He was a major.

"As you were!" He said.

I had been taught that "as you were" meant that I should immediately resume whatever I had stopped doing at the command "attention!" As I had been bending over picking blackberries when interrupted by the major I went back to that. It never occurred to me that this unimaginative major would wait there to be confronted squarely in the face with my rear end. Instead of saying something witty, he hit me over the bottom with the swagger stick. Caught off balance I fell head first into the prickly blackberry bushes.

Before I could get up, the major started down the road. I yelled after him, "I hope your war's a failure!"

His shoulders wiggled. He may have been amused. The important thing is that he didn't turn back, and I was free to continue eating those good wild French blackberries.

Buster's bad hearing nearly got him killed a few months later.

Late one night I had a narrow escape while coming back from a card game. A sentry challenged me, and I didn't hear his demand for the password or the two warnings he gave me after that. Then he pulled back the breach of his gun, prepared to shoot. My life was saved by my sixth sense which enabled me to hear that gun click—and stopped me dead in my tracks. After bawling me out the sentry listened to my explanation and got me past a second guard.

The Armistice was signed not long after Buster got to France, but like so many others, the men of Company C stood in a long line waiting to sail home. In the meantime Buster was sent to Bordeaux, where he and other theatrical types were ordered to form the "Sunshine Company," namesake of the 40th "Sunshine" Division. Bored soldiers needed entertainment. AEF commanders preferred that their men spend their time and money with YMCA volunteers rather than in French brothels where they could pick up syphilis or gonorrhea. The Y had scores of facilities across France and Italy where weary soldiers could take showers, write letters, play the piano, or even dance with American girls. Hundreds of American women came to France as Y volunteers, where, under careful supervision, they provided a taste of home for soldiers.

As a member of the Sunshine Company, Buster performed an old vaudeville act, the Princess Rajah—a fake "snake dance" with a string of sausages tied to a pole. An admirer sent word of his antics to the army brass, and Buster was invited to take his act all the way to headquarters. After the show, a general offered

American soldiers outnumber YMCA hostesses and wait their turn to dance with them. *Copyright unknown, courtesy of Harry S. Truman Library and Museum*

his car to return Buster to his quarters, and on the trip back, Buster talked the driver into helping him play a practical joke on his buddies, who were off duty and having themselves a fine time hanging out in a French village.

> None of the carousing privates, corporals, sergeants, and young officers there had seen a general for six months, and they all jumped to their feet as the car stopped before the hotel. The orderly got out and hurried around the car to open the back door for me. All over the square I could hear bottles dropping on the ground as the men and officers jumped up and came to attention. "My" orderly also stood at attention as I stepped out of the car in my dusty, wrinkled uniform. Over my shoulder I said, "I won't need you any more this evening."
>
> I was permitted to proceed unmolested for about 15 feet. Then the whole gang recognized me and let fly with curses, bottles, tomatoes, apples, and eggs. "You sonofabitch!" went up from hundreds of parched throats. I cut for the nearest alley, and thanks to my arduous stage conditioning got up enough steam to race out of town, where I slept peacefully throughout the night in a barn.

When he returned to the States after the war, Buster managed to get back to Hollywood, and his career soared. He scored big hits in film with comedies like *The General* (1927), *Steamboat Bill, Jr.* (1928), and *The Doughboys* (1930). Only Charlie Chaplin and Harold Lloyd could claim a place as Buster's competitors. His deadpan face and sheer physicality—plus the surprises he pulled off in his storylines—made him a hit with movie buffs of yesteryear and today. Buster Keaton worked very hard at his craft: to make people laugh. His last film appearance was in the 1966 comedy *A Funny Thing Happened on the Way to the Forum*. He died at his home near Los Angeles in 1966.

AFTERWORD

✴ ✴ ✴

"THE WAR TO END ALL WARS"

Throughout 1919 American soldiers, doctors, nurses, ambulance drivers, and entertainers sailed from France to pick up their lives at home and move on after the war. Americans stayed up to date on the war's aftermath by reading newspaper articles and photo magazines. Photographers, including the newly married Lucian and Helen Johns Kirtland, recorded impressive scenes of farewell ceremonies, as well as the far more solemn memorial rites for the fallen. The departing Americans left behind more than 53,000 US soldiers and officers who had died in France, their remains now laid to rest in eight military cemeteries.

The Great War had come to be thought of as "the war to end all wars" and "the war to make the world safe for democracy," but these visions were not to be. Only 20 years later, World War II would break out in Europe, and Americans would join the fighting in 1941.

In October 1918, the German government asked Woodrow Wilson to arrange terms for a balanced, peaceful end to

Lucian and Helen Johns Kirtland prepare for a photographic
journey over France.
Library of Congress,
LC-DIG-ppmsca-32777

the war. The American
president's Fourteen Points
laid out such a plan, and in
April 1919 Wilson sailed
to France to participate in
peace talks. But Wilson's
broadminded ideas were
abandoned during peace
talks in Versailles, in the
very palace where kings
and queens had once ruled France. The Allied nations demanded
"compensation by Germany for all damage done to the civilian
population of the Allies and their property by the aggression of
Germany."

The Treaty of Versailles exacted a huge toll on Germany in
the form of war reparations, a payment schedule of 269 billion
German marks—in gold, about 100,000 tons' worth. Moreover, the "guilt clause" in the treaty forced Germany to accept
all blame for the war, stirring up an already insulted German
public.

Woodrow Wilson's hopes for a just peace floundered. Germany's fledgling democracy failed to thrive with such a huge
drain on its economy, and in the early 1930s, many Germans
were attracted to the extreme politics of the National Socialist
(Nazi) Party and its mesmerizing leader, Adolf Hitler. By 1933
the Nazi Party had full control of Germany and, with government and the arms industry working hand in hand, began to

Lucian Kirtland captured
these images of American
cemeteries in France.
Edgar Allan Forbes, Leslie's
Photographic Review of
the Great War

build a fascist state. In March 1938 Germany annexed Austria
into its would-be empire, and in March 1939 Germany seized
Czechoslovakia. On September 1 the German army rolled into
Poland, igniting World War II.

As in the early years of World War I, many Americans held to their isolationist views and thought that Hitler was Europe's enemy to fight. But when Germany's ally Japan attacked the US Pacific Fleet at Pearl Harbor on December 7, 1941, the "sleeping giant" awoke and went to war. The United States and the Allied forces defeated both Japan and Germany in 1945.

This time, the victorious Allies—the United States, Britain, France, and the Soviet Union—divided Germany into two parts. The Soviet sector became communist East Germany; the western sector, the democratic West Germany. When the Soviet Union fell apart in 1989, East and West Germany reunited as the Federal Republic of Germany. Today, the German nation stands among the world's most successful democracies.

EPILOGUE

✶ ✶ ✶

When I was a kid growing up in Oak Park, Illinois, we once had a school assembly on Armistice Day. This was in 1963, after the holiday had been officially renamed Veteran's Day. Still, our teachers used that old-fashioned term: *armistice.*

A boy in our seventh-grade class was chosen to recite a poem on that November 11. I wasn't sure why. He wasn't the top student in our class of 50 kids, nor the best-behaved. But he had learned the poem by heart. He spoke softly and carefully, chin up and rather stiff, obviously coached by one of our teachers. His recitation made a huge impression on me that day.

The poem he recited, "In Flanders Fields," is the best known of the books, poems, and letters that came out of World War I. It was written in 1915 by a Canadian doctor-poet, John McCrae. The poem is both a memorial and a call to arms.

> *In Flanders fields the poppies blow*
> *Between the crosses, row on row,*
> *That mark our place; and in the sky*
> *The larks, still bravely singing, fly*
> *Scarce heard amid the guns below.*

We are the Dead. Short days ago
We lived, felt dawn, saw sunset glow,
Loved and were loved, and now we lie
In Flanders fields.

Take up our quarrel with the foe:
To you from failing hands we throw
The torch; be yours to hold it high.
If ye break faith with us who die
We shall not sleep, though poppies grow
In Flanders fields.

John McCrae never made it home to Canada. He died of pneumonia in a field hospital in France.

NOTES

∗ ∗ ∗

1. THE COWBOY: FRED LIBBY

All quotes in this chapter were taken from Fred Libby's book, *Horses Don't Fly*.

2. THE DAUGHTER: IRÈNE CURIE

"Dear Irène": Curie, *Madame Curie*, 289.
"Paris is calm": Curie, *Madame Curie*, 289.
"howl with laughter": Curie, *Madame Curie*, 284.
"Dear Irène, you know": Curie, *Madame Curie*, 292.
"A telegram or telephone call": Curie, *Madame Curie*, 295–296.
"The melancholy procession": Curie, *Madame Curie*, 296.
"From Montereau": Letter from Irène Curie to Marie Curie, July 7, 1916, *Musée Curie—Institut Curie*/CNRS.
"Mé chérie": Letter from Irène Curie to Marie Curie, September 13, 1916, *Musée Curie—Institut Curie*/CNRS.
"was met with": Pflaum, *Grand Obsession*, 212.

3. THE WORDSMITH: J. R. R. TOLKIEN

"If a boy employed": Carpenter, *Tolkien: A Biography*, 30.
"The usual kind of morning": Carpenter, ed., *The Letters of J. R. R. Tolkien*, 8.
"This miserable drizzling": Carpenter, *Letters*, 8.
"communication alleys": Carpenter, *Tolkien: A Biography*, 94.
"they were the Prussian Guard again": Carrington, *Soldiers from the Wars Returning*, 120.

"animal horror": Carrington, *Soldiers*, 94.

"15 July 1916": Carrington, *Soldiers*, 94–95.

"Ocean Villas": Garth, *Tolkien and the Great War*, 172.

"I suffered once": Carpenter, *Letters*, 54.

"My 'Samwise'": John Garth, "Sam Gamgee and Tolkien's Batmen," author's personal blog, February 13, 2014, http://johngarth.wordpress .com/2014/02/13/sam-gamgee-and-tolkiens-batmen/.

"One has indeed personally": Elizabeth Bruton, "JRR Tolkien, World War One Signals Officer," *Innovating in Combat: Telecommunications and Intellectual Property in the First World War*, http://blogs.mhs.ox.ac.uk /innovatingincombat/jrr-tolkien-world-war-one-signals-officer/.

5. THE AVIATRIX: KATHERINE STINSON

"As an aviator": "Katherine Stinson, Best of Women Pilots, Will Never Fly Again; Will Devote Self to Housewife's Duty," *San Jose Evening News*, August 2, 1928, 4.

"I enjoy flying.": "Flying as a Business Appeals to Seventeen Year-Old Girl, and She Will Join Professionals," *Cincinnati Enquirer*, May 5, 1912, 1.

"the little Southern girl": "BIPLANE: With Its Two Passengers Plunged to Earth Near the Coney Island Aviation Field—Occupants Escaped Injury," *Cincinnati Enquirer*, July 31, 1913, 8.

"The little aviatrice": "BIPLANE," *Cincinnati Enquirer*.

"the only one of her sex": "CERTAIN DEATH Predicted for This Young Lady, Who Is a Daring Aviatrix," *Cincinnati Enquirer*, September 10, 1916, 27.

"Katherine Stinson, who left Chicago": "Katherine Stinson Flies from Chicago to Binghamton, 783 Miles," *Aerial Age Weekly*, June 3, 1918, 580.

"I learned to drive a Ford": "The Reminiscences of Katherine Stinson," Columbia Center for Oral History Collection, July 1960, 43.

"contracted a heavy cold": "Ohio Troops Arrive," *Cincinnati Enquirer*, March 19, 1919, 9.

6. THE FAMILY: THE YOUNG ROOSEVELTS

"jolly naughty whacky baby": Edward J. Renehan, Jr., *Theodore Roosevelt's Family in the Great War* (New York: Oxford University Press, 1998), 85–86.

"hell yawned": Theodore Roosevelt, *America and the World War* (New York: Charles Scribner's Sons, 1915), 2.

"I don't go much in the wards": Betty Boyd Caroli, *The Roosevelt Women* (New York: Basic Books, 1998), 350.

"hero in the family": Brands, *T. R.: The Last Romantic*, 792.

"[A]ll four of us": Brands, *T. R.*, 793.

"From what I can gather": Roosevelt, ed., *Quentin Roosevelt*, 122.

"First there are no guns": Roosevelt, *Quentin Roosevelt*, 124–125.

"[T]he new service stripe regulations": Roosevelt, *Quentin Roosevelt*, 123.

Her French neighbors gossiped: Renehan, *The Lion's Pride*.

"There's no better way": Renehan, *Lion's Pride*, 121–122.

"There are some nice things": Renehan, *Lion's Pride*, 143.

"Baron von Richthofen": Renehan, *Lion's Pride*, 143–144.

"musical talent": Renehan, *Lion's Pride*, 165.

"More than eleven hundred thousand": "Pershing Has 1,100,000 Men," *New York Times*, July 14, 1918, 1.

"German and American activity": "German Machine Gunners Use Explosive Bullets in Fighting American Forces on the Marne," *New York Times*, July 14, 1918.

"Watch Sagamore Hill": Brands, *T. R.*, 797.

"But—Mrs. Roosevelt!": Brands, *T. R.*, 798.

"Quentin's mother and I": Brands, *T. R.*, 798.

"absolutely unconfirmed": Brands, *T. R.*, 798.

"The finest, the bravest": Brands, *T. R.*, 800.

"the final and definite announcement": Brands, *T. R.*, 800.

"poor, darling heartbroken": Brands, *T. R.*, 800.

"Then they could have had": Jennifer Greenwood, "Quentin and Flora," Official blog of the Theodore Roosevelt Center at Dickinson State University, July, 16, 2012, www.theodorerooseveltcenter.org/Blog/2012/July/20-Quentin-and-Flora.aspx.

"QUENTIN ROOSEVELT HAD SOLDIER BURIAL,": *New York Times*, July 21, 1918, 1.

"It is hard to open": "Theodore Roosevelt Sends a Letter of Deep Gratitude to Mrs. H. L. Freeland, Who Consoled Him After a Heartbreaking Loss," Andrew Carroll, ed., *War Letters: Extraordinary Correspondence from American Wars* (New York: Scribner's, 2001), 146.

"boy from Oyster Bay": "Quentin Roosevelt Had Soldier Burial," *New York Times*, July 28, 1918, 6.

"We'll start the war": William C. Meadow, *The Comanche Code Talkers of World War II* (Austin: University of Texas Press, 2009), 141.

7. THE RED CAP: HENRY LINCOLN JOHNSON

"Just three weeks' training": Little, *From Harlem to the Rhine*, 194.

"the German swore at him": Little, *Harlem to the Rhine*, 195.

"It started without traditions": Little, *Harlem to the Rhine*, 19.

The French called the black soldiers: Arthur Browne, "They Fought Like Hell—So He Could Fight Like Hell for His Country," *New York Daily News*, May 27, 2012, www.nydailynews.com/opinion /fought-hell-fight-hell-country-article-1.1084824.

"burning, stinging pain": Little, *Harlem to the Rhine*, 196.

"I feared that these men": Little, *Harlem to the Rhine*, 198.

"Two Black Yanks Smear": "Two Black Yanks Smear 24 Huns; Big Secret Out," *Stars and Stripes*, May 24, 1918, 1.

"he had been taken": Little, *Harlem to the Rhine*, 366

"notable instance of bravery": Casey Seiler and Tim Griffin, "Medal of Honor in Sight: Henry Johnson's Heroism Detailed in Communiqué," timesunion.com, March 22, 2011, www.timesunion.com/local/article /Medal-of-Honor-in-sight-1246522.php.

Henry's real name: Cindy Clayton/AP, "Medal of Honor Recipient's Story Finally Comes to Light," *Washington Post*, June 28, 2015, www .washingtonpost.com/local/medal-of-honor-recipients-story-finally -comes-to-light/2015/06/23/cb8e0e7c-19d9-11e5-bed8-1093ee58dad0 _story.html.

another family had stepped forward: Dan Lamothe, "How the White House and Media Got It Wrong on Medal of Honor Recipient Henry Johnson," *Washington Post*, June 11, 2015, www.washingtonpost.com/news/check point/wp/2015/06/11/how-the-white-house-and-media-got-it-wrong -on-medal-of-honor-recipient-henry-johnson/.

"devastating": Clayton/AP, "Medal of Honor Recipient's Story Finally Comes to Light."

8. THE PITCHER: CHRISTY MATHEWSON

"Big 6" "Matty" "Idol of All Fandom": "Matty, the Idol of All Fandom, Seriously Ill of Tuberculosis," *New-York Tribune*, July 31, 1920, 8.

"Mathewson pitched against Cincinnati": "Christy Mathewson," Baseball Hall of Fame, http://baseballhall.org/hof/mathewson-christy.

"endowed with extraordinary capabilities": Amber Roessner, *Inventing Baseball Heroes: Ty Cobb, Christy Mathewson, and the Sporting Press in America* (Baton Rouge: Louisiana State University Press, 2014), 136.

"We wound up drilling": Cobb, with Stump, *My Life in Baseball: The True Record*, 189.

"Baseball will never be": "French Regard Baseball 'Brutal' Says Mathewson," *New York Morning World*, February 18, 1919.

"Their infield work is rotten": "Baseball 'Too Rough' for French, Mathewson Reports," *New York Evening World*, February 19, 1919.

"At a hand signal": Cobb, with Stump, *Life in Baseball*, 190.

"Divine Providence": Cobb, with Stump, *Life in Baseball*, 190.

"when we were in there": Cobb, with Stump, *Life in Baseball*, 190.

"I saw Christy": Cobb, with Stump, *Life in Baseball*, 189.

"right hand man": Gurtowski, "Remembering Baseball Hall of Famers Who Served in the Chemical Corps," 3.

"He had a will": Gurtowski, "Remembering Baseball Hall of Famers," 191–192.

"Now Jane, I want": Paul Gillespie, "Christy Mathewson: The Christian Gentleman," *From Deep Right Field* (blog), January 15, 2013, http://from deeprightfield.com/christy-mathewson-the-christian-gentleman /#respond.

9. THE SHOWGIRL: ELSIE JANIS

"To the A.E.F.": Janis, *The Big Show*, vi.

"Boys, are we downhearted": James W. Evans and Gardner Ludwig Hardin, *Entertaining the American Army: The American Stage and Lyceum in the World War* (New York: Association Press, 1921), 74.

"I started in at home": Janis, *Big Show*, xi.

"was greeted by": Janis, *Big Show*, 4.

"The train would leave": Janis, *Big Show*, 91–93.

"Not because we": Janis, *Big Show*, 94.

"I leaned out quietly": Janis, *Big Show*, 135–136.

"Congratulations on your": Jennifer Keene, *World War I: The American Soldier Experience* (Lincoln: University of Nebraska Press, 2011), 62.

10. THE KID: ERNEST HEMINGWAY

"like a sharp smack": Baker, ed., *Ernest Hemingway: Selected Letters 1917–1961*, 14.

"[T]he road was having": Baker, *Selected Letters*, 15.

"the goddamnedest collection": Hotchner, *Papa Hemingway: A Personal Memoir*, 103.

"Shells aren't bad except": Hotchner, *Papa Hemingway*, 14.

"unlimited capacity": Villard and Nagel, *Hemingway in Love and War: The Lost Diary of Agnes von Kurowsky*, 21.

"Here lies the body": Villard and Nagel, *Love and War*, 17.

"Fresh and pert": Villard and Nagel, *Love and War*, 28.

"The Capt. walked": Villard and Nagel, *Love and War*, 62.

"Mr. Hemingway's birthday": Villard and Nagel, *Love and War*, 62.

"I have gone pretty far": Villard and Nagel, *Love and War*, 65.

"he tells me how much": Villard and Nagel, *Love and War*, 62.

"He 'lectured' Aggie": Villard and Nagel, *Love and War*, 66.

"Everything went beautifully": Villard and Nagel, *Love and War*, 68.

"in a manner": Villard and Nagel, *Love and War*, 28.

"Now, Ernest Hemingway": Villard and Nagel, *Love and War*, 72.

"Ernest Hemingway is": Villard and Nagel, *Love and War*, 72–73.

"I can't get away": Villard and Nagel, *Love and War*, 163.

"And I hope & pray": Villard and Nagel, *Love and War*, 163–164.

"You are a lost generation": Hotchner, *Papa Hemingway*, 49.

"Black-Ass": Hotchner, *Papa Hemingway*, 68.

11. THE CAPTAIN: HARRY TRUMAN

All excerpts from Truman's letters were found at the Harry S. Truman Library and Museum website, www.trumanlibrary.org.

"the first girl I ever": "Biographical Sketch of Mrs. Harry S. Truman," Harry S. Truman Library and Museum, www.trumanlibrary.org /bwt-bio.htm.

"blind as a stump": D. M. Giangreco, *The Soldier from Independence: A Military Biography of Harry Truman* (Minneapolis: Zenith Press, 2009), 5.

"tanned skin": "The Love Story of Harry and Bess Truman," National Archives, February 2004, www.archives.gov/calendar/features /2004/02.html.

"ever if she married": McCullough, *Truman*, 92.

"when Germany invaded": McCullough, *Truman*, 20.

"the fire from a battery": McCullough, *Truman*, 20.

"a colossal, all-out offensive": McCullough, *Truman*, 125.

12. THE COMEDIAN: BUSTER KEATON

All quotes in this chapter were found in Buster Keaton's book, *My Wonderful World of Slapstick*.

AFTERWORD

"compensation by Germany": "Peace Treaty of Versailles," Word War I Document Archive, http://net.lib.byu.edu/~rdh7/wwi/versa/versa7.html.

BIBLIOGRAPHY

✳ ✳ ✳

GENERAL INTEREST

Forbes, Edgar Allen, ed. *Leslie's Photographic Review of the Great War; Special Photographs by James H. Hare, Lucien Swift Kirtland [and others]; Explanatory Text by General John J. Pershing, President Woodrow Wilson [and others].* New York: Leslie-Judge, 1919.

Freedman, Russell. *The War to End All Wars: World War I.* New York: Clarion, 2010.

FRED LIBBY

Libby, Frederick. *Horses Don't Fly: A Memoir of World War I.* New York: Arcade Publishing, 2002.

IRÈNE CURIE

Curie, Eve. *Madame Curie.* New York: Doubleday, Doran, 1939.

Pflaum, Rosalynd. *Grand Obsession: Madame Curie and Her World.* New York: Doubleday, 1989.

J. R. R. TOLKIEN

Carpenter, Humphrey, ed. *The Letters of J. R. R. Tolkien.* Boston: Houghton Mifflin, 1981.

Carpenter, Humphrey. *Tolkien: A Biography.* New York: Ballentine Books, 1977.

Carrington, Charles. *Soldiers from the Wars Returning*. London: Hutchinson, 1965.

Garth, John. *Tolkien and the Great War: The Threshold of Middle-Earth*. Boston: Houghton Mifflin, 2003.

WALTER KOESSLER

Official website for *Walter Koessler 1914–1918*. http://walterkoessler.com/.

KATHERINE STINSON

Winegarten, Debra L. *Katherine Stinson: The Flying Schoolgirl*. Waco, TX: Eakin Press, 2000.

THE YOUNG ROOSEVELTS

Brands, H. W. *T. R.: The Last Romantic*. New York: Basic Books, 1997.

Renehan, Edward J., Jr. *The Lion's Pride: Theodore Roosevelt and His Family in Peace and War*. London: Oxford University Press, 1998.

Roosevelt, Kermit, ed. *Quentin Roosevelt: A Sketch with Letters*. New York: Charles Scribner's Sons, 1921.

HENRY LINCOLN JOHNSON

Little, Arthur W. *From Harlem to the Rhine: The Story of New York's Colored Volunteers*. New York: Covici, Friede, 1936.

Nelson, Peter. *A More Unbending Battle: The Harlem Hellfighters' Struggle for Freedom in WWI and Equality at Home*. New York: Basic Civitas, 2009.

CHRISTY MATHEWSON

Cobb, Ty, with Al Stump. *My Life in Baseball: The True Record*. Garden City, NJ: Doubleday, 1961.

Gurtowski, Richard. "Remembering Baseball Hall of Famers Who Served in the Chemical Corps." *Army Chemical Review*, July–December 2005.

Seib, Philip. *The Player: Christy Mathewson, Baseball, and the American Century*. New York: Four Walls Eight Windows, 2003.

ELSIE JANIS

Janis, Elsie. *The Big Show: My Six Months with the American Expeditionary Forces*. New York: Cosmopolitan Book Corp., 1919.

ERNEST HEMINGWAY

Baker, Carlos, ed. *Ernest Hemingway: Selected Letters 1917–1961*. New York: Charles Scribner's Sons, 1981.

Hotchner, A. E. *Papa Hemingway: A Personal Memoir*. New York: Random House, 1966.

Reynolds, Michael S. *The Young Hemingway*. New York: B. Blackwell, 1986.

Villard, Henry S., and James Nagel. *Hemingway in Love and War: The Lost Diary of Agnes von Kurowsky. Her Letters, and Correspondence of Ernest Hemingway*. Boston: Northeastern University Press, 1989.

HARRY TRUMAN

Harry S. Truman Library and Museum, www.trumanlibrary.org.

McCullough, David. *Truman*. New York: Simon and Schuster, 1992.

BUSTER KEATON

Keaton, Buster, with Charles Samuels. *My Wonderful World of Slapstick*. New York: Da Capo, 1982.

INDEX

✶ ✶ ✶